101 Things to Know Before Getting a Dog

Susan M. Ewing

lumina
MEDIA

Project Team
Editor: Amy Deputato
Copy Editor: Joann Woy
Design: Mary Ann Kahn
Index: Elizabeth Walker

LUMINA MEDIA™
Chairman: David Fry
Chief Executive Officer: Keith Walter
Chief Financial Officer: David Katzoff
Chief Digital Officer: Jennifer Black-Glover
Senior Vice President, Retail: Scott Coffman
Vice President Content: Joyce Bautista-Ferrari
Vice President Marketing & PR: Cameron Triebwasser
Managing Director, Books: Christopher Reggio
Art Director, Books: Mary Ann Kahn
Senior Editor, Books: Amy Deputato
Production Director: Laurie Panaggio
Production Manager: Jessica Jaensch

Library of Congress Cataloging-in-Publication Data
Names: Ewing, Susan M.
Title: 101 things to know before getting a dog : essential considerations to
  prepare your family and home for a canine companion / Susan M. Ewing.
Other titles: One hundred and one things to know before getting a dog
Description: Irvine, CA : Lumina Media, 2016. | Includes index.
Identifiers: LCCN 2016042858 (print) | LCCN 2016043012 (ebook) | ISBN
  9781621871231 (softcover) | ISBN 9781621871248 (ebook)
Subjects: LCSH: Dogs. | Dog adoption.
Classification: LCC SF427 .E947 2016 (print) | LCC SF427 (ebook) | DDC
  636.7/0887--dc23
LC record available at https://lccn.loc.gov/2016042858

This book has been published with the intent to provide accurate and authoritative information in regard to the subject matter within. While every precaution has been taken in the preparation of this book, the author and publisher expressly disclaim any responsibility for any errors, omissions, or adverse effects arising from the use or application of the information contained herein. The techniques and suggestions are used at the reader's discretion and are not to be considered a substitute for veterinary care. If you suspect a medical problem, consult your veterinarian.

lumina MEDIA

2030 Main Street, Suite 1400
Irvine, CA 92614
www.facebook.com/luminamediabooks
www.luminamedia.com

Printed and bound in China
19 18 17   2 4 6 8 10 9 7 5 3 1

Contents

Introduction
First Things First...

In this book, I use the masculine pronoun when talking about dogs, unless I'm speaking about a specific dog whose sex I know. When I speak of breeders, I use the feminine pronoun because female breeders seem to be in the majority. I try to write to a specific person, but because a first-time dog owner could be anyone, I've tried to cover all the bases, whether the reader is a twelve-year-old getting a puppy, a parent trying to select the right family pet, or the senior who wants a canine companion. Also, because the new dog could be a puppy or an adult, I've tried to cover both possibilities. Generally, advice for a puppy can be translated into advice for an adult dog, but an adult dog may learn certain things faster from past experience.

Why 101 things? Years ago, there was a list making the rounds that went something like this:

- All you need to show a dog is a dog and a leash and a collar.
- All you need to show a dog is a dog and a leash and a collar and a tack box full of grooming supplies.

> …and a grooming table.
>
> …and an ex-pen.
>
> …and so on.

The list continues with all of the extras, culminating in a motor home. It was a humorous look at all of the items you can accumulate because of your dog—many useful but not strictly necessary.

This book is like that list. You might not need to buy or think about all 101 things, but they're good to know about anyway, and they'll help give you the best beginning to a lifelong friendship with a dog.

Initial
Considerations

Thinking It Through 1

and visit the litter box if you're going to be home later than expected. When you're ready to relax on the couch and watch television, a cat isn't in going to get in your face, pleading for a game of fetch or a brisk hike in the rain. A cat will be more willing to just curl up in your lap and let you get your fur fix. And, while cats can certainly enjoy the company of other cats, they're more likely to be content on their own, especially if they have a window seat and can watch the wildlife in your backyard.

Maybe a hamster or a gerbil would be more your style. They're both furry and cute, but with a full water bottle and some food, they can be left on their own much of the time. Gerbils don't even need their cages cleaned that often.

How about some fish? An aquarium requires an initial investment in a tank, filters, and heaters, and you do need to clean it occasionally, but, for the most part, once you've established your fish, you just need to remember to add food once or twice a day. Beauty, variety, and limited care.

If you want something cuddly but don't really want to do much work to take care of that something cuddly, maybe a stuffed animal would fit the bill. There are some terrific stuffed animals out there, and they don't shed, make noise, or eat. Years ago, pet rocks were a fad. Maybe a lovely piece of granite on a shelf would meet your need for

Do you really want a dog? This is the very first question you should ask yourself. You may think you want a dog for many reasons: you had a dog as a child, you think your children should have a dog, you like your friend's dog, and so on. Try to go beyond these thoughts. If you're the couch-potato type or are rarely ever home, maybe some other pet would suit you better. All animals need attention, but some need more than others.

Cats don't need daily walks around the block, and they can munch some dry food something decorative, and it would require only dusting now and then.

Why a Dog?

Unconditional love is one of the things that make dogs so popular. No matter what happens at work, no matter how dysfunctional your family, your dog will love you. Burst into tears, and there's that faithful friend, trying to lick your face and make it all better. A dog will never criticize your taste in clothes or suggest that you lose a few pounds.

Don't forget, though, that even unconditional love requires work. A dog doesn't take care of himself. He needs food, medical care, shelter, and playtime. If you don't have the time and money to provide what he needs, you're back to a stuffed toy.

Does Everyone Want a Dog?

"Please, can we get a dog? Please, please, please?" If this sounds like your child, the next phrase out of his or her mouth will likely be, "I'll take care of him! I promise." This isn't true, of course. No matter how much a child says it, or even believes it, the truth is that one or both parents will be responsible for the dog's care. You can either accept that fact and agree to take on the extra work or convince your child that a stuffed dog is way better than a real dog.

It's not enough that the child(ren) in the family wants the dog. Based on unscientific research, I'd say that nine out of ten children polled would vote for a dog. However, the entire family must want the dog. It's not fair to the dog if one family member dislikes him and ignores or, worse, abuses him. It's not fair to the dog if there's no primary caretaker. Kids will agree to anything to get a dog, but they are still kids, which means that they'll forget to put down clean water, or feed the dog on time, or give him his daily walk. It's up to an adult to make sure that the dog receives proper care, and that's less likely to happen if the adult in charge didn't really want the dog to begin with. This is why a dog should never be a surprise gift. Unless your best friend has been insisting that a Golden Retriever would make her life complete, or you know that Aunt Sally can't live without a Pomeranian, give a box of chocolates instead.

Consider what size dog you should get. You may have your heart set on a Great Dane or a St. Bernard, but if you live in a studio apartment, that may not be the best choice. While most large breeds are fairly docile and do not have extensive exercise needs, you'll want everyone to be comfortable, so consider how much room a specific dog will take up and how much room that leaves you. On the other hand, some small dogs, such as Parson Russell Terriers, are very energetic. With any dog, size isn't the only consideration; you must factor in the dog's exercise needs as well.

Also think about what type of coat a dog has. If you've always wanted to be a hairdresser, a dog who needs frequent grooming may be your perfect choice. For example, Poodles, whether in show coat or puppy trim, need to be clipped every four to six weeks. Taking the dog to a professional groomer will save you some work, but the costs can add up. Whether you buy grooming equipment and learn to do it yourself or make regular visits to a groomer, you can't let grooming slide. Even many shorter coated breeds have double coats and shed heavily twice a year, and you'll need to brush all that dead fur out. Dogs with softer coats and no undercoat, like Lhasa Apsos and Shih Tzus, need to be kept in short puppy clips or be combed out daily to prevent mats.

All dogs need their nails trimmed on a regular basis. If you live in the city and walk your dog frequently on pavement, his nails will wear down and may not need as much manual clipping. There are several types of canine nail clippers on the market if you want to do it yourself, or you can visit a groomer. Generally, nails need to be clipped every four to six weeks.

Male or female? You may or may not have a preference. Both sexes can be loving, loyal companions. Depending on the breed, males may be significantly larger, so that may be a consideration. Some people find males to be more independent and females to be more willing to please, but this may be something that shows up in a particular breed or family line rather than a trait that has anything to do with gender.

With the particular line of Pembroke Welsh Corgis that I've had, the males have always been less inclined to obey than the females. And if I were upset for some reason, the females seemed more concerned—one of my males would go so far as to run upstairs and hide if I was crying. None of this made any difference in the amount of love I felt for them.

Some people would rather have a female because of the male's tendency to lift a leg and mark territory. Neutering helps lessen this behavior in males but may not stop it entirely.

When it comes to temperament, all dogs are different in terms of personality, and there are differences within breeds, depending on parentage and how the dogs were raised, but you can make certain generalizations about breeds that will help you decide which breed might be best for you. If you are interested in a mixed breed, it's helpful to know what breeds are in the mix.

All reputable breeders strive for even temperament in their dogs. This means that, regardless of breed, breeders want dogs who are confident and not shy or fearful. Any well-socialized dog will face new experiences calmly, but a dog's breed has more bearing on whether a dog will be wary of strangers or happy to kiss everyone. For example, many working dogs may have been bred to guard and protect, so these breeds will be less likely

to be effusive in greeting strangers—at the same time, they shouldn't be so fearful or defensive that they attack.

If you have a large family and active household, with a lot of friends coming and going, a Golden Retriever might be a better choice than, say, an Akita. That's not to say that you can't have both an Akita and an active social life, but you may need to put in more time training and socializing that Akita.

Poodle in show clip

People tend to think of puppies when they think about getting a dog, but there are many reasons why an adult dog might be a better choice. For one thing, if you get a puppy, be prepared for sleep deprivation. Until your puppy has grown a bit, you will have to get up and get your puppy out quickly when he needs to go. It doesn't take forever for him to "hold it" through the night, but it can feel like it! If you're young and have a young family, then you'll already be used to not sleeping through the night, so getting a puppy won't be as disruptive. Also, puppies are clueless. You need to take the time, and have the patience, to work with your puppy until you understand each other.

You may not know the background of an adult dog, but an adult is likely to have a working knowledge of basic commands, such as Sit, Stay, and Come. An adult dog will probably be housetrained; even if he is not, he will learn more quickly than a puppy. An adult dog may also be totally up to date on his vaccinations, which will reduce the initial cost of bringing home your new dog.

Puppies spend a lot of time exploring and, like toddlers, they tend to put much of what

Adult and puppy Bernese Mountain Dog

> ### A DOG'S VOCABULARY
> There are many things I did not set out to purposely teach my dogs, but they've added many words to their vocabularies on their own. They know what I mean when I say "Do you want to go out?" Or "Do you want some cheese?" Or "Stop that!" They know to head for their crates when I say "kennel" … and lots more besides.

they find in their mouths. You need to puppy-proof your home, just like you would for a child. Older dogs are much less likely to poke into every cupboard, although if they smell something enticing, all bets are off.

Puppies teethe. That means nothing is safe from tiny teeth. This may work as an incentive for your family to keep the house tidy. Otherwise, shoes and slippers are fair game, as are towels, shirts, blankets, and pillows. My most recent puppy found a bit of loose wallpaper in the kitchen and enjoyed chewing and tugging on it. Well, I was planning to redo the kitchen anyway!

My first Corgi puppy found and chewed the corner of a treasured book. That was the day I asked myself, *Which do you value more, the book or the puppy?* The puppy won, but if you have something you would hate to see damaged by teeth marks, put it out of your puppy's reach. If the puppy chews the leg of a chair, you may appreciate the memories that chair brings back when your dog is gone. If the chair's an antique, put it in the attic until the dog's an adult.

Adult dogs are past the teething stage, so your belongings are relatively safe. An adult dog might occasionally chew something forbidden, but it shouldn't be an everyday occurrence. All of her adult life, one of my Corgis would destroy any pencil she found unattended—nothing else, just pencils.

Digging is another activity that seems to be puppy-related. Terriers, of course, will dig throughout their entire lives because it's what they were bred to do, and terrier owners must accept that. All types of puppies seem to enjoy digging, though. If you have an immaculate lawn or garden, you may want to reconsider

NEW ROUTINES

Some people feel that an older dog will come with more "baggage" than a puppy. While it's true that the older dog will have gotten used to particular routines that may or may not be part of your own routines, he is still able to adapt to a new home and lifestyle.

that stuffed animal. Or, you can designate an area of the yard for digging and teach your dog to dig there and nowhere else. An easy way to create such an area is to get a kiddie wading pool and fill it partway with dirt or sand. You can encourage your dog to dig in it by hiding a few treats and special toys just under the surface. If the dog loses interest, just reseed with tasty treats.

An older dog may not be as playful as a puppy. Unless you lead a very active lifestyle, though, less playful may be a good thing.

Getting an older dog doesn't mean that you can't still have a specific breed, if that's what you're looking for. Just research your breed-specific rescue. If you don't care about getting a purebred, your local shelter is just the place. Or, check out Petfinder.com, where you're likely to find a variety of purebred and mixed-breed dogs.

Age—Yours, Not the Dog's

You need to consider your age just as much as the dog's. Having a puppy is a lot like having a child in that it's much easier when you're young. As much as you hear that "60 is the new 40," and as good as you feel and as healthy as you think you are, trust me— when it comes to raising a puppy, 60 is the new 70. Had I given it more thought when we got our last puppy, I would have adopted an older dog.

Is it Hot (or Cold) in Here?

Even with central heat and air conditioning, it's still a good idea to think about your area's climate before you choose a dog. Sure, you

can live in Florida and share your home with a Siberian Husky or an Alaskan Malamute, or you can live in Wisconsin with an American Hairless Terrier, but you might have to make more adjustments than if you had considered climate first.

Northern breeds were bred to have thick double coats to protect them from snow and cold. Giving one of these breeds the

Young Siberian Husky

exercise they need and want in a hot-weather location can be a challenge. Sure, you can exercise your dog early in the morning and in the evenings when it's cooler, but if you live near Phoenix, Arizona, for instance, "cooler" may mean 80 degrees in the summer. For a dog bred to be active, staying indoors most of the time isn't fair.

And that American Hairless Terrier? He's not going to be happy in the snow. You'll need nice warm sweaters and probably booties as well. You may think that you'll enjoy dressing your dog, but imagine doing it at least three to five times a day when your dog needs to go out. And, you certainly can't let your dog out into your yard and forget him. When we have sub-zero temperatures, my Pembroke Welsh

LITTER TRAINING

If you choose a small short-coated or hairless dog in a cold climate, an option is to train your dog to do his business indoors, in a litter box. It's a workable solution, but think about it ahead of time. If you don't like the idea, consider a different type of dog.

Corgis get cold feet within three minutes of going out, and a short-coated or hairless dog has an even smaller window of time for outdoor activity in winter weather.

Couch Potato or Triathlete?

Another thing to consider is your activity level and that of your family. A Dalmatian may be the perfect dog for you if you like getting out every day for a 5-mile run. If you prefer to collapse into your favorite chair after a day at work and want a dog who will be happy to watch television with you, select a toy breed or possibly one of the smaller non-sporting breeds. All dogs need exercise, though, so no matter what size or type of dog you choose, never forget that he needs attention and some activity.

And don't think you can base energy level on the size of the dog. A Saint Bernard can be happy with less exercise than a smaller terrier or herding dog. A Greyhound needs a good race around your fenced yard once or twice a day, and then he will willingly join you on the couch until it's time to go to bed—and he will happily join you there, too!

CHECK FIRST!

Always check with your landlord before you get a dog; if you haven't discussed whether pets are allowed, don't just assume that your landlord will permit a dog. Maybe your landlord is fine with dogs, but only smaller ones. Check your lease and speak to your landlord in person about any restrictions. Your landlord may require an additional security deposit to cover any damage or have certain rules about use of the yard. If you already know that your landlord does not allow dogs, don't try to sneak one in. The landlord will find out, sooner or later, and it's the dog who will pay the price. It would be terrible if you bought or adopted a dog and then couldn't keep him. Ask first!

Two other very important questions you must ask yourself before getting a dog—right up there with "do I want a dog at all?"—are "am I prepared for the expense of owning a dog?" and "how much time do I have to devote to a dog?" According to the AKC website (www.akc.org), in 2015, two veterinary students totaled the first year's costs for small-, medium-, large-, and giant-breed puppies. Keeping in mind that expenses for the first year are likely going to be higher than average (puppies eat more, first shots, spaying or neutering), the numbers can be intimidating. The results are as follows: "The average cost for the first year of raising small dogs was $2,674; medium dogs, on average, cost $2,889; the cost for large dogs is $3,239; and giant breeds, such as Great Danes, have an annual cost of $3,536."

The students figured in one serious illness per year, but many dogs go year after year without needing more than just their annual checkups. Still, other costs, such as training, beds, toys, and fencing, are not included in these numbers.

Keeping in mind that small dogs live longer than large or giant dogs, you will be responsible for your dog for approximately ten to eighteen years. After the excitement and the newness wear off, are you prepared for the long haul? It's easy to fall in love with a puppy, but be honest—will you love him just as much when he's an adult? Will you love him when he's old, slow, and possibly incontinent? Will you love him when the veterinary bills start adding up? How about when you have to pay extra for special food or medicines?

Dogs typically cost more at both ends of their lives. As your dog ages, he may need medicine for arthritis. He may need to have some teeth pulled. He may need a more expensive senior-formula or prescription food. Maybe you'll need to buy a ramp if he can no longer manage stairs.

On the bright side, dogs are cheaper than children. Obedience lessons are cheaper than college, and your dog won't be asking for a car, the latest smartphone, or an expensive pair of shoes. Even so, consider the expenses. If your budget can't stretch another penny, or if you'd rather save your money for a world cruise, you're back to a stuffed animal or a pet rock.

It's OK to not want a dog to begin with. It's not OK to mistreat or

abandon a dog when he's no longer a cute puppy or when he causes you extra work. But, that's not you. You want a dog and are prepared to take care of him for life. If you've never had a dog, maybe you don't realize how much time that dog may need.

Puppies, of course, take a lot of time. Many breeds housetrain very quickly, but while a puppy is being trained, someone has to be there to make sure he is taken out on a regular schedule. If you leave home at 7:00 in the morning and are gone for twelve hours, you'll need to make arrangements for someone to take care of your puppy during the day.

The dog's age also plays a part in how much time and attention your new friend will need. Younger dogs are typically more active and have more energy. They're also more likely to be destructive if left alone. They get bored, are full of bounce, and may decide that the woodwork makes an ideal chew toy. If they're teething, then almost anything is fair game for easing the itchy, achy feeling of new teeth coming in.

Some breeds need more exercise no matter what their age. If you're giving that Dalmatian a good long run twice a day, fine. If you don't have the time and energy for that, choose a breed that's happier with a stroll around the block.

If you love spur-of-the-moment getaways, maybe you should rethink getting a dog. You can't just take off for a long weekend without making arrangements for your dog, whether that's a boarding kennel, a pet sitter, or taking the dog with you. If you take the dog with you, you have to first make sure that he is welcome wherever you're going. Will you want to take the time to pack everything you will need for your dog?

Dogue de Bordeaux puppy

A noisy dog will do nothing to endear you to your neighbors.

Some people let their own nationality factor into their choice of dog. Someone with Scottish ancestry may select a Scottish Terrier or a Scottish Deerhound, for example. When my father finally got a dog, I think his Welsh heritage played a part in his choosing a Pembroke Welsh Corgi. However, nationality should not be the sole reason for your choice; you must still pick a dog whose traits you like and who will be compatible with your lifestyle.

Allergies may also play a part in the selection process. One of the reasons Poodles and Poodle crosses are so popular is that they may be hypoallergenic. Note the word "may." No dog is totally hypoallergenic, and some dogs that cause a problem with one person may be fine with another. Three breeds that are typically considered possible choices for those who are allergic to most dogs are Poodles, Portuguese Water Dogs, and Kerry Blue Terriers, because they have coats that are closer to hair than fur. These breeds don't shed, but they need to be trimmed regularly.

Allergic reactions in some people may have more to do with whether or not there's an undercoat. Single-coated dogs, like the Maltese, Shih Tzu, and Yorkshire Terrier, may be just fine for the allergy sufferer.

THE RIGHT DOG FOR EVERYONE

Dogs have been companions to people for thousands of years, and they range in size from Chihuahuas to Irish Wolfhounds. They have short hair, long hair, and no hair. Some bark a lot, and others rarely make a sound. With a little research and effort, you can find the perfect dog for your situation—but take time to do that research! It's easy to fall in love, but if there's not some thought behind it, it's just as easy to fall out of love.

Years ago, a woman got in touch with me for information about Pembroke Welsh Corgis. She had researched several breeds, and the Corgi was one of the breeds that fit her criteria for a pet. Her concern was that she was allergic to some dogs, but not others, and she didn't want to get a dog and then find out she was allergic. At the time, I had five Corgis, so I invited her over to see what would happen. It wasn't long before she was sneezing and her eyes and nose were running. She continued her search and eventually got a Parson Russell Terrier, which worked out very well for her. Each person is different.

Do you mind if a dog is noisy? If you own your own home, it might not matter if your dog barks at every leaf that falls, but if you're in an apartment, a quiet dog will keep relations friendly with other tenants.

Golden Retriever

Scottish Terrier

A purebred puppy from a breeder will most likely cost more initially than adopting a dog from a rescue or shelter. Pet-quality puppies often, but not always, cost less than show quality puppies. Some breeders charge the same price for all puppies because the same care goes into producing each puppy in the litter. "Pet quality" just means that, in the breeder's opinion, the dog is not likely to win in the show ring. The puppy may have an undesirable marking or a physical trait that only a show judge would notice, such as a shoulder angle that's not quite up to the breed standard. A dog should not be deemed pet quality because of any health issue. In fact, purchasing from a reputable breeder may even save you money on veterinary bills in the long run because genetic problems likely won't show up later in your dog's life.

Prices for purebred dogs cover a wide range. Generally, rare breeds will cost more because the supply is limited. Breeds that produce larger litters may be cheaper than breeds that typically only produce one or two pups in a litter. Conversely, if a breed becomes popular rapidly—for example, because of a movie (think *101 Dalmatians or Beethoven*)—the price may go up because people are willing to pay for the privilege of owning a "celebrity" breed.

Even within a breed, prices can vary depending on the part of the country you're in or what an individual breeder feels she can reasonably charge. You may be willing to pay more if you're working with an expert breeder with a stellar reputation.

Australian Shepherd puppy

St. Bernard puppy

Labrador Retriever puppy

Rescue and shelter dogs will also cost something, even if just for spaying or neutering and necessary vaccinations. Many rescue organizations will charge an adoption fee to help defray the costs of housing, feeding, and veterinary visits for the dogs in their care.

What happens if you've found the perfect dog from a breeder or rescue, but he's 500 miles away? Are you willing to make the trip to get that dog? The Internet has made it easy to look at and compare multiple dogs from all over the country, but once you've made your choice, you need to get your dog. If you'll want to pick up your dog in person, think about how far you're willing to travel before you fall in love. In some cases, shipping or a rescue transport may be possible, but the logistics are not always simple.

If you're picking up the dog yourself, will the seller be supplying a crate, or will you need to buy one before you make the trip? Are you crossing state lines, entering another country, or staying in a campground overnight? Make sure that you have all of the necessary paperwork for traveling with your new pet.

If you're asking a breeder or a rescue group to ship your dog, know your options. If the dog will be shipped by air, check the airline regulations. Many airlines limit the number of animals they will accept on any given flight. If the flight has a connection, or a stop,

where will the dog be during that stop? Also, most airlines will not ship an animal if the temperature is below 45 degrees F or above 85 degrees F at the originating airport, at your destination, or anywhere else the plane is scheduled to land. You'll also need an airline-approved crate for shipping, so that's an extra expense.

Some rescue groups have teams of volunteers who will help transport dogs to their new homes, but because the date of the transport is dependent on the schedules of those volunteers, you may have to wait longer than you'd like for your dog, and you may still need to drive a distance to get to the transport stop nearest to you. Some rescue organizations charge a fee to reimburse the volunteers for gas and travel costs, while others do not—in the latter case, you should consider making a donation to the rescue anyway.

Adopting a mixed breed comes with the initial expense of adoption fees or a donation.

There are approximately 200 breeds of dog recognized by the American Kennel Club (AKC), with more on their way to recognition each year. The AKC categorizes breeds into seven regular groups—Terrier, Toy, Hound, Working, Herding, Sporting, and Non-Sporting—based on what the breeds were originally bred to do. An eighth group, the Miscellaneous Class, comprises breeds who have lower numbers in the United States and are in the process of proving their viability. Worldwide, there are more than 400 recognized breeds! So, you've got a wide field to choose from.

Terriers are generally high-energy, fearless dogs who were bred to "go to ground"— a.k.a. dig—to catch prey. Toy breeds were created as portable companions. Hounds were originally part of the Sporting Group and are further classified as scenthounds or sighthounds based on their hunting style. Working dogs were bred to haul loads, act as guards, or protect livestock. Herding breeds were bred to herd livestock, moving them from place to place. The Sporting Group contains dogs that were bred to find game and, in many cases, retrieve it. The Non-Sporting Group covers a wide range of dogs, from Boston Terriers to Dalmatians, who were originally bred for specific jobs that no longer exist. If you want a dog for a specific purpose, like ridding a barn of vermin, herding a flock of sheep, or retrieving ducks, studying the dogs in the appropriate group will help you find the right dog for the job.

One reason for choosing a purebred is that you want to compete in events that allow only purebreds. Years ago, I attended a dog show and was fascinated by the dogs in the obedience ring. I wanted to do that, too. At the time, we had a mixed-breed dog, and competitive events were open only to purebreds. After some research, I got our first Pembroke Welsh Corgi. Times have changed, and, while you still need a purebred to compete in conformation shows, mixed breeds can now compete in performance events.

Another reason you might choose a purebred puppy or dog is that you know

Dalmatian puppy

CONSISTENCY IN BREEDING

Don't discount purebreds because you've heard that mixed breeds are healthier. Reputable breeders work hard to produce dogs that are sound physically and mentally, and they take advantage of the health tests available for their breeding stock. That doesn't guarantee that a purebred won't have a problem, but it's a good start.

exactly what you are getting as far as size, weight, coat, and, to some extent, temperament. There's no guesswork involved. A Corgi puppy will not grow to be 3 feet tall and weigh more than 100 pounds. A Chihuahua will remain lap-sized. A St. Bernard will be large and furry and will drool. A sporting breed should be willing and able to help you find and retrieve game. If you live in a rural area, a terrier can help control the rodent population.

Reliable breeders will know what health problems are likely to occur in their breeds and will test their breeding stock in an effort to eliminate, or lessen, the chance of that problem occurring in their litters. They breed not only for good health but also for temperament, and they socialize their puppies, giving them the best start possible before the puppies go to their permanent homes. A reliable breeder will offer a contract, spelling out the agreement between the breeder and the buyer, and the breeder will take that dog back at any stage of the dog's life, for whatever reason. No reputable breeder wants a dog she's bred to end up in a shelter.

Beagle adult and puppy

A PUREBRED'S "PAPERS"

Generally speaking, purebred dogs in the United States will be registered with either the AKC or the United Kennel Club (UKC). Depending on where you live, you might have access to dogs registered with the Canadian Kennel Club (CKC). When I was growing up, a dog that "had papers" was considered superior to other dogs, and you might still consider it a point of pride to have a registered dog, but keep in mind that registration with any recognized organization just means that the dog's parents were both of the same breed. Registration is no guarantee of quality. The parents could be lovely examples of the breed, or they could be oversized, mismarked, cow-hocked, genetic disasters whose offspring could still be registered (although a reputable breeder would not use poor-quality dogs for breeding).

An unscrupulous breeder can breed brother and sister together—as long as they are the same breed, the puppies may be registered. Or, that same breeder could breed two dogs with no genetic testing and produce a litter with a congenital illness. So, do your homework on breeders. A responsible breeder will ensure that the quality is there, along with the registration papers.

Note that not all breeders are reputable. They may not know or care about hereditary health issues when they match up dogs for breeding. They probably won't worry about which puppy is best for which home. Reputable breeders try to do their best for both the dog and the buyer, but it's also up to you, as a buyer, to protect your own interests. The more you know about your chosen breed, the better prepared you'll be to get the very best dog for you.

A reputable breeder is the best way to get a quality puppy if you think you'd like to show your dog in conformation. Experienced breeders are generally able to tell the difference between a show-quality puppy and one with some minor fault that would prevent him from winning at a conformation show.

You may have your heart set on rescuing a dog, and that's great! Even purebreds need to be rescued. If you've fallen in love with a particular breed but aren't interested in showing and don't care if you have a puppy or adult, check out the rescue organizations that exist to help that breed. Purebreds also end up in shelters.

Further on, you'll see pages devoted to each of the AKC groups of purebred dogs. Take a look at them. Even if you decide on a mixed breed, knowing a bit about what might have gone into that mixed breed may save you from choosing the wrong dog.

There are several good ways to search for your new purebred best friend. Start by visiting the American Kennel Club's website at www.akc.org or the United Kennel Club's website at www.ukcdogs.com. On these websites, you'll find information on the national clubs—also called parent clubs—of the organization's registered breeds. Your chosen breed's parent club can help you find a breeder.

A local kennel club in your area may also be able to put you in touch with a breeder. Or, attend a dog show. Dog shows are a great way to see many different breeds all in one location. If a particular breed catches your eye, talk to the handler about what the breed is like to live with.

If you decide to attend a dog show, there are some things to keep in mind. First, morning is a great time to see obedience or agility, if these events are part of the show. Second, unless it's a benched show, of which there are very few, people may leave after they've shown. Get a judging schedule or check InfoDog online (www.infodog.com) if you want to know when a specific breed will be shown. If you're interested in Corgis, for instance, and they are being shown at 8:00 a.m., don't

Watching an agility event lets you see some energetic breeds in action.

go at 11 a.m. with hopes of talking to Corgi people.

Finally, ask when you can talk to someone about your chosen breed. If a handler is busy grooming or rushing to the ring, he or she is likely to be abrupt because the main concern at that moment is showing, not talking. Once the judging is over, you'll find that most dog people are happy to talk to you and answer questions. This is an excellent way to learn about a breed's temperament, energy level, and grooming needs.

If you're doing a general online search for a purebred, rather than looking at breeders you found through a reputable registry, such as AKC, the UKC, or a parent club, beware. Not all those who have websites are good breeders; they may just be fancy puppy mills. If a site offers more than two breeds, that's a red flag.

Boxer puppy

If the site says that the breeder always has puppies, that's another red flag. Reputable breeders plan their litters carefully and rarely "always" have puppies.

Beware of anyone claiming to have "rare" examples of a breed. "Rare" frequently means "more money," and "rare" is not always a good thing—there is probably a reason that a particular trait is rare. As an example, in Pembroke Welsh Corgis, a longhaired Corgi is called a "fluffy." This is a fault that would count against the dog in the show ring. A recessive gene causes the fluffy coat, and breeders try to avoid producing fluffies. For that reason, a fluffy is "rare." A fluffy makes a perfectly good pet for someone willing to groom the longer coat, and it's acceptable to sell such a dog as a pet. It is not acceptable, however, to ask for more money because the dog is "rare." In

RARE BREEDS
Certain breeds are considered rare. The Norwegian Lundehund, for example, is a rare breed in the United States because there aren't very many registered Lundehunds in the country.

another example, a "rare" all-white Boxer may be deaf.

Avoid dogs being sold as "teacup." Some dogs are supposed to be tiny, but the "teacup" designation is not used in the standard of any breed. In some cases, dogs have been bred down to such a small size that health problems multiply and their life spans may be drastically shortened.

You may also find a specific breed in a rescue organization or at a shelter. In these cases, you won't know if the dog has been tested for genetic diseases, and you won't be able to see the parents or any siblings. However, adopting from a rescue or shelter is a great way to bring home your chosen breed while giving a deserving dog a second chance at a good home.

Yorkshire Terrier puppies

10 Interviewing a Breeder

If you've decided on a purebred, you'll have to choose a breeder. You'll want to talk to the breeder and ask her any questions you have about the breed, and the breeder will have questions for you, too. At first, it may seem like a good breeder doesn't want to sell any of her puppies because she will start off by telling you everything negative about the breed. Yes, she wants to sell the puppies, but she wants them to go to good homes and to people who are ready for the pros and cons of that particular breed.

Using Corgis as an example, they shed a lot, they bark—some more than others—and they can be stubborn. If you want peace and quiet and very little shedding, a Corgi wouldn't be the right choice. If you treasure your perfectly landscaped yard, a terrier, with his instinct to dig, may not be a good choice. Newfoundland and St. Bernard breeders may warn you that when the dog shakes his head, you could end up with drool on your walls and maybe even your ceiling.

Don't fall so in love with a breed that you ignore the negatives. You will be living with that dog for upward of a decade. Be prepared.

For your part, ask about any hereditary diseases and if the parents have been tested for these problems. Don't believe a breeder who says she never needs to test her dogs because they are all perfect.

If you are looking at a puppy, ask to see the mother of the litter as well as all of the puppies. You may not be able to see the father if he doesn't live with the breeder. Your breeder may select the puppy she thinks best fits your lifestyle, but you should still be allowed to see all of the puppies and the mother. If the facilities aren't clean or if any puppy looks ill, find another breeder.

A good breeder will have many questions for you before she agrees to sell you one of her puppies. For example, a breeder will likely ask if you've ever had a dog before and, if so, what happened to him. If you say you've had five dogs who have all been hit by cars and killed, the odds are good that you won't get a dog from this breeder. The breeder will also want to know if you've ever owned this specific breed before. Not every breed is right for every person or family.

The breeder will ask about your yard and whether it's fenced. She'll ask how you plan to exercise your dog. She'll ask if you own or rent your home. She'll ask if you have children and, if so, how old they are. Be honest with your answers. Your breeder wants the best for both you and the dog, and she may be able to give you advice on the best way to exercise your dog or how to teach your children to respect the dog. Breeders want everyone, human and canine, to be happy, and they've learned what questions to ask and what the best responses to those questions are.

A reputable breeder will have a sales contract that spells out just what is being offered and what each of you promises. For instance, a contract may say that the puppy,

DOGS AND KIDS

Generally, breeders of toy dogs don't like to place them in homes with children under five years of age, who may not fully understand how gentle they must be with a dog. Sometimes breeders of giant breeds have the same restriction because a clumsy, playful puppy that weighs 40 or more pounds could inadvertently injure a small child.

depending on his age, has already had certain vaccinations. It may give you a window of time, anywhere from forty-eight hours to two weeks, for you to have the puppy examined by a veterinarian. If the doctor finds anything seriously wrong with the puppy during this time frame, you may be able to return the puppy to the breeder for either a refund or a replacement puppy. The contract may require you to spay or neuter the puppy at a specified age and to show proof of the procedure to the breeder. The contract will also say that the breeder will take the dog back at any time. Responsible breeders are responsible for the dogs they breed for the dogs' entire lives.

Sometimes, a breeder will offer co-ownerships. Breeders frequently do this with show-quality dogs because they want to get their kennels recognized for their quality.

Such a breeder may make showing the dog a condition of ownership and may sign the dog over to you once you've put a championship or performance title on the dog. In other cases, the contract may specify that the breeder gets to breed the dog and, if the dog is a female, to keep a specified number of the puppies before signing over ownership.

Co-ownership contracts may mean a lower price initially and can be beneficial to both parties, but think carefully before you agree to a co-ownership. If there are conditions such as showing or breeding, are you interested in spending the time and money to show a dog? Do you want to deal with a female in season until it's time to breed her? If something goes wrong, then what?

A PERFECT MATCH

The breeder's questions are not meant to prevent you from getting a dog; rather, they are a tool to make sure that you get the right dog.

The bottom line is that contracts are designed to protect both parties, but you need to understand the terms. If you don't like the terms, and you and the seller can't agree, it's time to look for another reputable breeder.

One advantage to a mixed breed is that the initial cost will be lower. When you buy a purebred puppy from a reputable breeder, you are paying for all of the health checks and careful study that went into the breeding. You are paying for a known commodity as far as size, amount of fur, activity level, and general temperament. With a mixed breed, you may not be able to meet either parent. You won't know if the puppy is carrying the genes for progressive blindness or whether he is predisposed to hip dysplasia.

Unless someone has intentionally bred two purebreds to create a mixed breed, like a Goldendoodle, or you know who the puppy's parents were, there's no way to know what a mixed-breed dog's background is unless

you have a DNA test done. Before spending some time with the dog, you won't know if he will be protective, or love water, or have a tendency to bay at the moon.

Try to find out as much as you can about a mixed-breed puppy or dog. Rescue groups usually put their dogs in foster homes, where they are able to live in a family environment, which may include children, other dogs, or other pets. In this way, the rescue is able to learn about the dog's traits and behavior. In shelters, volunteers are often able to tell how a dog reacts to other dogs or to cats as well as the people who visit the shelter to look at the dogs.

If you've fallen in love with a roly-poly puppy and you don't care how much fur he'll have as an adult or whether he'll grow up to weigh 14 or 40 or 140 pounds, go ahead and follow your heart. Mixed breeds offer just as much love, fun, and companionship as any purebred can and can even enjoy most of the performance events that a purebred can.

While there may be pet stores with healthy, well-socialized puppies, most pet store stock comes from puppy mills, where the only concern is cranking out "product." It's best to steer clear. Besides not having any health checks and possibly being the product of tight inbreeding, many puppies end up being in the store well past the optimal time for socialization. Some may be months old before they ever even set foot on grass. You may be buying both health problems and temperament instabilities when you buy from a pet store, and most pet stores offer no guarantees and won't take back a puppy once he's sold. Pet-store puppies frequently cost more than healthy puppies from reputable breeders, and the pet store will not be there to answer questions and guide you like a breeder or rescue volunteer would.

Many pet *supply* stores, however, do open their doors to shelters and rescue groups, giving them a chance to showcase their available animals, and that's a good way to meet several dogs of different ages, sizes, and energy levels.

Shelters are full of dogs, both purebred and mixed breed, whose original owners didn't take the time to research what kind of dog would be best for their families. They fell in love with puppies who grew too big or too hairy or too active. If you're actively looking for a dog, visit your local shelter on a regular basis because new dogs come in frequently. If you're looking for a specific breed, ask if they'll call you if they ever get that breed in. A friend of mine did just that and ended up with the Dalmatian he wanted.

While most dogs in shelters are adults, you may find puppies from time to time. The drawback to getting a mixed-breed puppy from a shelter is that, while you may be able to guess at the puppy's lineage, you won't really be able to tell how big or small the dog will be as an adult.

Another drawback with shelters is that your selection may be limited. Even if you'll be perfectly happy with a mixed breed, you may still have preferences as to size, coat type, or activity level. Small, cute dogs are the first to get adopted. Black dogs are frequently last. Depending on your region, pit bulls and pit bull crosses may be in the majority at your local shelter. Pit bulls can make wonderful pets for those who want an active, strong, short-coated dog. If you're looking for something smaller and fluffier, you may have a long wait before the dog of your dreams is at the shelter.

Some shelters network with other area shelters to help a wider range of dogs find homes. Some shelters may also have foster homes that take in dogs to learn more about their personalities, such as whether they are good with other dogs, with cats, or with children. The shelter itself may work with the dogs to do some temperament testing and learn more about them. Our local shelter has a "test cat" that they use to determine how a dog will react to cats, but not all shelters do that. If you have small children or other pets, you need to consider this before you adopt.

Animal shelters may not have many adoption requirements, but shelters are typically overcrowded and may not know too much about the available dogs unless they've had volunteers spend time with the dogs. Author Caroline Coile, writing in *ShowSight* magazine (March 2016) says, "While many

LOOK ONLINE

Many shelters and rescue groups post dogs available for adoption on the Internet. Some popular sites are Petfinder.com, Adoptadog.com, and Petcha.com. Using these sites, you can check out adoptable dogs all across the country. Click on a dog that interests you, and you'll get more information about that dog, including how to contact the group that has him.

fine dogs come from shelters, it is truly a case of adopter beware. Adopters should ask about a dog's history, reason for surrender, and, if possible, should talk to [the] former owner. Caveats such as 'doesn't like men/women/children' or 'has nipped on occasion' or 'must have experienced owner' may be red flags."

Sometimes dogs are surrendered to shelters complete with veterinary records and registration papers, if applicable, but this is not the norm. However, sometimes the shelter can find out something about the dog's background from the person surrendering the dog.

IN THE MIX

Our first dog came from a shelter, and we were told that she was a St. Bernard/German Shepherd Dog mix. I think that was pretty accurate, but at that time, I didn't realize that giant breeds like St. Bernards take about two years to fully mature. I thought that, at six months, Ginger was about as big as she'd get. I was wrong. Had I done a little research on giant breeds, I'd have known that Ginger was going to keep growing. It didn't matter to us that she finally topped out at 110 pounds, but someone else might have returned her to the shelter.

Dogs end up in rescue for many reasons. One reason may be that the former owners didn't research the breed. They may have fallen in love with a cute puppy (and what puppy isn't cute?) and found out as the puppy grew up that the breed was too big or too hairy or too noisy. Sometimes, older people are just not able to care for a dog anymore, and that dog may end up in rescue. Some people just give up on a dog when he reaches adolescence or when he chews up one too many pairs of shoes (which could have been avoided by putting shoes out of the dog's reach).

There are many rescue groups who focus solely on one breed or type of dog (e.g., giant breeds, senior dogs) as well as rescues who take in purebreds and mixed breeds, adults and puppies, and large and small alike. A rescue group may cover a large area, such as an entire state or multiple states, and there are also smaller, more local, groups. In my area, there's a rescue group that takes in only hounds, mainly Beagles and Beagle crosses. Another small rescue takes in all breeds.

If you're looking for a purebred, and you don't know of any local rescues, visit the AKC's website to find information for that breed's parent club; almost all AKC parent clubs have a rescue component or can refer you to a breed-specific rescue group. Some parent clubs list all of the rescue organizations connected with their breed; with others, you can contact the national rescue volunteer to find groups in your area. Find the one closest to your home and start there.

There may be some conditions and will likely be a contract involved with adopting from a rescue group. Most rescue groups start out by having you fill out an application so that the rescue understands what type of dog you're looking for and learns about what type of home you can provide for a dog. Once you're approved for adoption, you'll get into the specifics of what dogs are available for adoption and which one(s) might fit well into your family. If the rescue has no good matches for you at that time, they will contact you when a suitable dog enters their rescue.

The rescue may ask your preference as to sex, color, and age. If you have a preference. answer honestly. It may seem shallow to say that you want a red Corgi and not a tri-color, but for a successful adoption, both you and the dog have to be happy.

On one rescue application I saw, potential adopters were asked how they would handle a specific behavior problem. If questions like this come up, don't be afraid to say that you don't know or that you'd find a professional trainer to help. Professional trainers are professional for a reason. They've seen, and dealt with, many problems, some of which may be beyond the knowledge of the average pet owner.

A basic question that is on all rescue questionnaires (and shelter applications, too) is whether you rent or own your home. If you rent, you may be asked to provide a letter from your landlord stating that you are

allowed to have a dog and that no restrictions would prevent you from having the particular type of dog in which you are interested.

With many rescue groups, the dogs awaiting adoption spend time in foster homes, allowing the rescue volunteers to evaluate them in a home environment. You'll know before you adopt if the dog likes other animals, is good with children, or is a couch potato. Rescue groups want their charges to go to forever homes, and they work hard to make the best matches possible.

Many dog breeds traditionally have their tails docked and/or their ears cropped, with reasons rooted in history. Centuries ago, people thought that docked tails prevented rabies. In the 1700s, in Great Britain, there was a tax on working dogs with tails, so many breeds were docked to avoid the tax. Further, many working, herding, and sporting breeds had their tails docked to prevent tail injuries in the field. Terriers frequently had their tails docked so that the remaining length would provide an easy handhold if the dog needed to be pulled from a burrow.

Tails may be docked at various lengths. In the United States, Pembroke Welsh Corgis' tails are cut so that very little tail is in evidence, Boxers' tails are docked to a short stubs, and Poodles' tails are docked to $\frac{1}{2}$ to $\frac{2}{3}$ of the original length. Breeders generally dock tails when puppies are just a few days old.

These days, there's no tax related to a dog's tail length, and many people feel that a natural tail helps a dog with balance when turning sharply or when swimming. Studies have shown that dogs with shorter tails are at a disadvantage when interacting with other dogs because it changes their body language.

Ear cropping is done to give erect ears to dogs with drop ears

Adult Doberman Pinscher with cropped ears.

and was frequently done on fighting dogs so that there was less for their adversary to grab. Upright ears also tend to give the dog a more alert and, at times, more intimidating look. A Doberman with drop ears looks more like a lovable hound than an alert guard dog. Boxers and Great Danes are further examples of dogs whose ears are traditionally cropped in the United States. Ears are cropped between seven and twelve weeks of age.

Many people today question whether docking or cropping is necessary. Some countries have banned the practices, and even some people dedicated to conformation showing leave tails long and ears natural in case they want to show in another country or sell puppies abroad.

If you adopt through a rescue group or are searching shelters for your dog, you probably won't have a choice when it comes to whether a dog of a particular breed has a docked tail or cropped ears. If you have your heart set on a traditionally docked or cropped breed but want a puppy with a natural tail and ears, you'll need to find a good breeder who is willing to work with you, and you'll need to make those arrangements before the expected litter is born. Whatever your opinion on docking or cropping, it's another thing to think about when you're choosing a dog.

17 Health Benefits for Dog Owners

As you're considering adding a dog to your family, do you realize all of the positive aspects of dog ownership? Your dog will never talk back, never crash the car, never borrow anything without asking, never want the latest in clothing or shoes, and never need money for college—and, with a dog, you will never eat alone. Those benefits alone should make it understandable why people have dogs, but there are also measurable health benefits to having a dog.

Study researcher Allen McConnell of Miami University in Ohio was quoted in a July 11, 2011, article by Jennifer Welsh on LiveScience.com: "Specifically, pet owners had greater self-esteem, were more physically fit, tended to be less lonely, were more conscientious, were more extroverted, tended to be less fearful, and tended to be less preoccupied than nonowners."

A March 18, 2015, article by Katie Golde on Greatist.com titled *The 11 Science-Backed Reasons You Need to Get a Puppy (Right Now)* notes several benefits. According to researchers at the American Heart Association, having a dog can reduce your risk of getting cardiovascular disease. Part of this is probably because dog owners may get more exercise, and it's also been proven that petting a dog lowers a person's blood pressure.

Because dogs are nonjudgmental and offer unconditional love, they make great therapists, whether by just listening to you

vent about your bad day at work or in a formal capacity as therapy dogs, visiting hospitals, nursing homes, and schools as well as helping veterans with post-traumatic stress disorder (PTSD). In her book *Reporting for Duty: True Stories of Wounded Veterans and Their Service Dogs* (Lumina Media, 2015), Tracy Libby documents case after case of veterans who, after the physical and mental damage inflicted by war, are able to live productive lives with service dogs by their side. Dogs help veterans with PTSD function socially by offering a sense of protection and by using their bodies to block people from coming too close so that the veteran doesn't feel threatened. Many service dogs are trained to jump on or nudge their owners when they detect a change in breathing or heart rate that signals the onset of anxiety. In this way, dogs can end a nightmare or bring a person back to the present if he or she is having a flashback.

Many therapists have discovered that having a dog in the office helps patients open up. Even Freud had his Chow Chow in the office with him. In her article, Golde says that, at Miami University, "Students can take advantage of pet therapy that alleviates feelings of homesickness and depression. Dogs

WORK BUDDY
An article in *Time* magazine, March 3, 2016, noted that people who took their dogs to work were much less stressed, but still got just as much work done.

are on call during midterms and finals, when those feelings are at an all-time high."

Dogs may even be instrumental in helping people quit smoking. In the UK-published journal *Tobacco Control* in February 2008, a study indicated that if people were informed about the dangers of secondhand smoke to their pets, they would be inclined to stop smoking or have others refrain from smoking in their homes.

Studies have shown that children with dogs in their families develop fewer allergies as they grow up and also miss fewer days of school (and they can always claim that the dog ate their homework!).

Dogs also help their owners meet people. Going to the dog park can be a great way to meet other dog owners, not to mention joining a local kennel club or competing in a dog-related event. You may also make new friends in your neighborhood when you're out taking your dog for a walk.

18 Working Dogs

Most of the dogs in the AKC's Working Group were bred to do a job. For the most part, they are large, big-boned dogs. Many have been bred to be suspicious of strangers, and they may also be fearless, ready to stand up to a charging boar or a wolf intent on stealing a lamb. German merchants used Rottweilers as "walking banks"—they'd tie their moneybags around their dogs' necks, and it would be a very foolish thief who would try to steal that money.

If you have very small children, keep in mind that a working-dog puppy could accidentally injure a toddler. Conversely, once a working dog understands his role in the family, he will be a protector. This can be both good and bad, as he can perceive other children as a threat when they are simply playing with your children. If you think you want a dog from the Working Group, study the particular breed(s) that interests you to make sure it's a good fit with your family.

The Alaskan Malamute, the Siberian Husky, the Chinook, and the Samoyed were all bred to work in very cold climates. Their thick double coats keep them warm, even in below-zero temperatures. They are probably not the best choices for those living in southern Arizona, but they might be very happy in Maine. Also, all of these breeds need plenty of exercise and may also be happier outdoors than inside. These breeds are less likely to be as wary of strangers, but they can also be very independent. They were bred to run and pull, not to be attentive to human direction.

Samoyed

The Anatolian Shepherd, the Komondor, and the Kuvasz are examples of dogs bred to guard flocks of sheep. Originally, they lived with their flocks and were fierce defenders of the sheep. They may be very wary around strangers. If you have lots of people coming and going in and around your home, and you choose one of these breeds, your dog will need to be well-socialized—even then, he may not greet strangers with a smile and a wagging tail.

Some working dogs, like St. Bernards, Newfoundlands, and Bernese Mountain Dogs, were bred to work with people, so they're more laid back and more likely to be happy to make new friends. They also have thick coats, so if you're not comfortable with the idea of lots of fur floating through your home, you'd better think of a different breed.

Most working breeds are not as active as some of the other breeds, so if you're looking for a purebred jogging companion, you might look elsewhere. One exception is the Doberman Pinscher, who is sleeker than many of the others and could certainly keep you company on your morning run.

The Portuguese Water Dog has a curly coat, more similar to a Poodle's. That's good news on the shedding front, but you'll need to factor in the cost of either regular grooming appointments or the proper tools if you choose to groom your dog at home. The Standard Schnauzer and the Black Russian Terrier are two other dogs in this group who will need more than just a good brushing now and then.

POPULARITY
Some of the most popular dogs in the Working Group are the Boxer, Siberian Husky, Doberman Pinscher, Great Dane, and Mastiff.

Some of these large dogs drool a lot. The St. Bernard, the Newfoundland, the Mastiff, and the Neapolitan Mastiff are on the top ten list of droolers. If one of these dogs shakes his head, you could end up with drool on your ceiling—but many people live happily with these dogs in spite of the drool. The dog may not have access to the entire house, or the family may just always have towels handy to wipe the dog's muzzle. Some people only consider the traits they love in these breeds. Other people may not be able to get past the drool. It's just something to consider before you get the dog.

Boxers are great family dogs, with lots of energy for almost any kind of play, and they also make good watchdogs. They have a sense of humor, but they can also have a stubborn streak. Boxers are prone to several types of heart disease, including cardiomyopathy, and they are susceptible to bloat. Find a reputable breeder who has tested the parents for heart problems. Their life span is eight to ten years.

Siberian Huskies are friendly, happy dogs who get along with just about everyone, including other dogs, although they may consider smaller pets prey. They need a lot of exercise, and they're good at scaling fences or digging underneath, so make sure that your yard is secure. Ask the breeder if the parents have been screened for hip dysplasia and for progressive retinal atrophy, an eye condition. The breed's life span is about twelve years.

Doberman Pinschers are sleek, elegant dogs who are very loyal and who seem to have a keen ability to sense when someone is a threat. They need regular exercise as well as training. An untrained Doberman is likely to become destructive. Health concerns include cardiomyopathy; von Willebrand's, a bleeding disorder; and cervical vertebral instability (CVI), sometimes called Wobbler's syndrome. Healthy parents do not guarantee that your dog will not develop a genetic disorder, but it increases the odds of good health. The Doberman's life span is about ten years.

Great Danes are massive, short-coated dogs, weighing between 110 and 190 pounds. They are sweet, gentle dogs, but because of their size, they need to be trained not to jump up or to be at all aggressive. They need only moderate exercise, so if your own tendency is toward being a couch potato, you won't have to change your lifestyle too much. Health concerns include hip dysplasia, bloat, and cardiomyopathy, and their life span is about seven years.

Mastiffs weigh in between 120 and 230 pounds, so be prepared for some serious strength. They are gentle dogs, but because of their size, they cannot be allowed to jump up or to pull on a leash. They drool, especially after eating or drinking, so be prepared to wipe their muzzles. If you're anti-drool, choose another breed.

Health concerns include hip and elbow dysplasia, heart disease, bloat, and several eye conditions. Cystinuria is a genetic kidney defect. Life expectancy is about eight years.

Young Giant Schnauzer

SOME OF THE AKC'S HERDING DOGS ARE:

- Australian Cattle Dog
- Australian Shepherd
- Belgian Malinois
- Belgian Sheepdog
- Belgian Tervuren
- Berger Picard
- Border Collie
- Bouvier Des Flandres
- Cardigan Welsh Corgi
- Collie
- German Shepherd Dog
- Icelandic Sheepdog
- Miniature American Shepherd
- Old English Sheepdog
- Pembroke Welsh Corgi
- Pyrenean Shepherd
- Shetland Sheepdog
- Spanish Water Dog

There is a big range of sizes within the Herding Group. Considering how many smaller dogs are in this group, it's obvious that size isn't a consideration when herding livestock. Smaller stature may even be a plus. In fact, it's easy for short-legged Pembroke Welsh Corgis to duck under the hooves of a kicking cow.

The dogs in the Herding Group are intelligent and make good competitors in performance events. They were bred to take direction but also to think for themselves when needed, so many herding breeds have been used as military dogs and service dogs.

None of these breeds is an incessant barker, but herding dogs will definitely bark to sound the alarm. You will always know when the mail carrier has arrived or if there's a strange animal in the yard.

Most of the herding breeds are good with children and have enough energy to enjoy extended play sessions. The ones with longer legs will also make good jogging companions. Some of these breeds have a tendency to "herd" anything that moves, and this may mean children. The dog may instinctively chase and nip at heels, which could frighten a child. Monitor playtime, and make sure that children understand the dog's behavior.

Further, some herding breeds may want to keep everyone in a group. A Border Collie, for instance, may try to keep children together rather than letting them run in different directions. I had a Corgi who hated to see a person move from one room to the other; he wanted everyone to stay seated in the living room.

There are a variety of coat types in this group. Many of these dogs have double coats, which serve them well in all weather conditions. Some,

Rough Collie

GROOMING
Generally, while some herding dogs may require more grooming than short-coated breeds, it is grooming that you can do yourself, without too many trips to a professional.

like the Collie and Shetland Sheepdog, have long outer coats as well as dense undercoats. Even the Belgian Malinois and the Australian Cattle Dog, both of whom appear to have short coats, still have thick undercoats.

Some breeds have more than one variety of coat. For example, there are smooth- and rough-coated Collies, and the Pyrenean Shepherd has the rough-faced variety, with longer, harsher, woollier hair that may cord; and the smooth-faced variety, which has much shorter hair on the muzzle and overall has softer, finer fur that is no more than 3 inches long on the body.

The Berger Picard has a harsh, rough coat. If you saw the movie *Because of Winn-Dixie*, you saw a Berger Picard. The Bergamasco has an entirely different coat, made up of three separate layers: the undercoat; the long, straight, rough "goat hair;" and the woolly, finer outer coat. The goat hair and the outer coat twist together to form flat sections of felted hair known as "flocks." Each flock is 1–3 inches wide, and they are never combed out.

Yet another coat type is found on the Spanish Water Dog; this breed has a single curly coat. When longer, the coat can form cords, similar to those of a Puli or Komondor. Traditionally, in Spain, these dogs were clipped once a year and their coats sheared just like a sheep's.

Speaking of the Puli, the breed's corded coat takes considerable work because those cords need to be carefully formed. If you've fallen in love with a Puli, you may want to consider keeping him in a puppy clip. However, if the cords are part of what you love about the breed, work with your breeder to create and keep the hundreds of cords.

Among the most popular dogs in the Herding Group are the German Shepherd Dog, the Australian Shepherd, the Shetland Sheepdog, the Pembroke Welsh Corgi, and the Collie. German Shepherd Dogs have been popular ever since Rin Tin Tin made it big in Hollywood. This breed is versatile and highly intelligent. It is also very protective of its family and will definitely warn strangers to be careful. These dogs need plenty of exercise and training. Health concerns include hip dysplasia, degenerative myelopathy (spinal-cord disease), epilepsy, vision problems, immune-mediated diseases, and digestive problems. The breed's life span is ten to thirteen years.

Australian Shepherds are active, friendly, easy-to-train dogs that make great family pets. Name a sport—obedience, agility, herding—and Aussies can excel. They need lots of exercise, but they learn quickly and love to work. They'll be happy to play ball for as long as you want to. Health concerns include hip dysplasia and several eye diseases, and they can be affected by multiple drug sensitivity (MDS), which causes a risk of fatal reactions to a number of common veterinary drugs. Fortunately, there's a simple test for this. Their life span is twelve to sixteen years.

The Shetland Sheepdog is another wonderful, versatile breed, weighing just under 30 pounds. They have a lot of coat, but if you don't mind a dust bunny or two (or more!) of fur, you're fine. The Sheltie is rather vocal, but that makes him a good watchdog. He's fairly active, which is good news if you want to try performance events. The Sheltie might not be the best breed for very small children, but it is generally a good family dog. Health concerns include hip dysplasia, Collie eye anomaly, progressive retinal atrophy, von Willebrand's, and dermatomyositis (DM), also known as Sheltie skin syndrome. The average life span is twelve to fourteen years.

Pembroke Welsh Corgis are smart, active dogs who are always ready to play and are good with children and with other pets. They are not incessant barkers, but they will definitely let you know if someone's at the door or if another dog just walked by the house. They shed heavily twice a year, so be prepared for the hair! Their short legs disqualify them as jogging partners, but they're great at obedience, rally, agility, and herding. Health concerns include progressive retinal atrophy, von Willebrand's, and degenerative myelopathy. Tests are available for the latter two, so ask your breeder to see the health clearances on your prospective puppy's parents. If your breeder did not perform these tests, find another breeder. The breed's life span is twelve to fourteen years.

Collies come in rough-coated (think Lassie) and smooth-coated varieties. The smooth coat is short, but both varieties have and undercoat, and both shed. Collies are good family dogs and are happy to participate in any game or sport. Health concerns include bloat and a range of eye diseases, including Collie eye anomaly and progressive retinal atrophy. The Collie's average life span is ten to twelve years.

Pyrenean Shepherd

20 Toy Dogs

You've come to the right group if you want a small, portable dog who just wants to cuddle and be your friend. Coat types in this group include almost totally hairless, short, long, and curly. With the exception of the terriers in the group, who still display a terrier temperament, the dogs in this group were bred as companions. Whether you prefer the sleek good looks of an Italian Greyhound or a Manchester Terrier, the stocky body of the Pug, or the abundant locks of the Pekingese, this group has it.

The more delicate of these breeds are not recommended for households with small children, and none of these breeds was made for rough-housing, but if you're looking for a dog who doesn't need much exercise and will happily be your couch buddy, choose a toy breed, but just be aware that toy dogs can take longer to housetrain. When many of these breeds were developed, housetraining just wasn't much of an issue. It was too easy to clean up after such a small dog— or, in castles and palaces—to just ignore it altogether.

Yorkshire Terriers are among the most popular of all AKC breeds. These petite terriers have long, silky steel-blue coats with tan points. The Yorkie's coat requires daily care, even if clipped short, so consider the grooming requirements before adding a Yorkie to your home. Weighing between 4 and 7 pounds, Yorkies are spunky and playful, as well as lovely. As with many small breeds, Yorkies are susceptible to patellar luxation (a condition in which the kneecap slips out of place), dental issues, hypothyroidism, and Legg-Calve-Perthes disease, which slows the blood supply to the head of the thighbone. Very small dogs and puppies may also suffer from low blood sugar, or hypoglycemia. The breed's life span is twelve to sixteen years.

The Poodle typically ranks among the AKC's top ten most popular breeds, and Toy Poodles certainly make delightful companions and are just as lively and intelligent as the larger varieties (Miniature and Standard, members of the Non-Sporting Group). While they may not have the size to retrieve ducks, they can learn tricks and, if obedience or agility appeals to you, your little Poodle will be happy to join you. Health concerns include luxating patellas, Addison's disease, Cushing's disease, and hypothyroidism. The overall lifespan is fourteen to eighteen years, with Toy Poodles likely to reach the far end of this range.

The popular Shih Tzu has a long double coat that you can easily keep in a puppy trim. This sturdy little dog weighs between 9 and 16 pounds and makes a good watchdog—but once you let a new person inside your home, the Shih Tzu is all about love. Health concerns include dental problems, luxating patellas, and progressive retinal atrophy. Shih Tzus are also prone to renal dysplasia, a disease in which the kidneys don't develop normally. This condition can be inherited, so make sure the breeder has had the parents tested. Shih Tzus have large, front-facing eyes that can easily be injured. Life expectancy in the breed is from ten to eighteen years.

It's a hard-hearted person who can resist the big brown eyes and soft expression of the Cavalier King Charles Spaniel. This lovely little spaniel weighs between 10 and 18 pounds and wants to be with you no matter what you're doing. He's happy to go for a long walk, participate in a doggy activity, or just curl up next to you for a snooze. While Cavaliers can live from ten to fourteen years, they unfortunately are susceptible to a heart disease called mitral valve disease. This condition can be controlled with medication, but there is no cure. Cavaliers may also have syringomyelia, a nervous-system disorder that causes fluid-filled cavities in the spinal cord, resulting in pain and sensitivity in the head and neck. Syringomyelia may be managed with pain medicine or corrected with surgery, but it may also be so severe that the dog must be euthanized.

The Pomeranian has been bred down from about 30 pounds to its current size of 3 to 7 pounds, but it's still a charming, high-energy spitz-type dog. That thick double coat needs attention in the form of thorough brushings, but that's about it. Poms make good watchdogs; if you want a silent companion, keep looking. They're probably not the best with children because of their size. Besides the luxating patellas and dental problems common in toy breeds, Poms may have collapsing tracheas, which makes wearing a collar problematic. They are also susceptible to skin problems. The lifespan is fifteen years or more.

Italian Greyhound puppy

21 Sporting Group

THE AKC'S SPORTING GROUP INCLUDES:

- American Water Spaniel
- Brittany
- Chesapeake Bay Retriever
- Clumber Spaniel
- Cocker Spaniel
- Curly-Coated Retriever
- English Cocker Spaniel
- English Setter
- English Springer Spaniel
- Flat-Coated Retriever
- German Shorthaired Pointer
- German Wirehaired Pointer
- Golden Retriever
- Irish Setter
- Irish Water Spaniel
- Labrador Retriever
- Nova Scotia Duck Tolling Retriever
- Pointer
- Spinone Italiano
- Vizsla
- Weimaraner
- Welsh Springer Spaniel

The Sporting Group is the oldest AKC group, consisting largely of dogs used for hunting, specifically fowl. Some of these dogs were bred to retrieve waterfowl and thus may have webbed feet along with a high tolerance for diving into cold water. Others were bred to point and/or flush birds on land and then retrieve the fallen game. Many of these dogs, such as the Vizsla and the Weimaraner, are very high-energy dogs, needing lots of exercise. Most sporting dogs were not bred to curl up on the couch with you—not that many of them aren't happy to do just that, but only after a long day in the field or after some other strenuous exercise. Other sporting dogs, such as the Clumber Spaniel, Sussex Spaniel, and Cocker Spaniel, are a bit more laid back. Almost all of the sporting breeds are friendly and ready to play, and if you live near water, they'll love going for a swim. If you're a hunter, you can't go

wrong with one of these breeds; if you enjoy competition, there's not much that these dogs can't do.

There are a variety of coat types in this group, but none needs much professional care unless you're planning to show your dog. Cocker Spaniel coats have gotten thicker and longer in the show ring, but if you aren't showing your Cocker, you can keep his coat much shorter.

The Labrador Retriever has been the number-one breed in terms of AKC registrations for decades, and it's easy to see why. Labs have short, easy-care coats and come in black, chocolate, and yellow. They are family-friendly and, at 55 to 80 pounds, are sturdy enough to enjoy a bit of roughhousing with children. They'll happily play fetch for hours, join you for a swim, or retrieve a duck. Most are good with other pets as well. Hip and elbow dysplasia are a concern, as is progressive retinal atrophy, and some Labs may be susceptible to skin allergies. Life expectancy is ten to thirteen years.

It's no surprise that Golden Retrievers are also among the top AKC breeds. There's more grooming involved with the long golden coat, which can range from a pale yellow to a deep gold that's almost red, but you can do the brushing yourself. Goldens love people and are willing to please, making them popular in the obedience ring. Like the Labrador, they'll play for hours and then be happy to curl up at your feet. As long as they can be near you, they're happy.

Unfortunately, many different types of cancers seem to attack Goldens, and heart disease, specifically subaortic stenosis, is also prevalent, so you should have your dog's heart checked annually. Hip and elbow dysplasia are common. The breed's life span is ten to twelve years.

The German Shorthaired Pointer is a popular, good-looking, energetic dog with a short, close coat in liver and white. These dogs need exercise, so they're good choices for joggers. If you can't give them the exercise they need, you'd better choose another breed. They make good watchdogs because they are protective and will let you know if they think something's suspicious. They weigh between 45 and 70 pounds.

While hip dysplasia can show up in any breed, it is less prevalent in the German Shorthaired Pointer than in many others. Reputable breeders will perform DNA testing for an eye disease called cone degeneration to ensure that they do not pass this disease on. Some German Shorthaired Pointers experience entropion, a condition in which the eyelid turns inward, causing the eyelashes to scratch the cornea. Fortunately, this can be corrected with surgery.

The Brittany, at 30–45 pounds, is an easy-to-groom bundle of love who is eager to join in just about any activity. A Brittany

Vizsla **puppy**

will enthusiastically jog, play fetch, or race with you around an agility course. If you're a hunter, he will happily be your partner in the field. As a bonus, the breed's white-and-orange or white-and-liver coat makes it a handsome addition to the family. Health concerns include hip dysplasia, hypothyroidism, and cataracts, and the breed's life span is between twelve and fourteen years.

If you want joy and bounce in your dog, another good choice is the English Springer Spaniel. Weighing 35–50 pounds, the Springer can be an active partner in the field, on your daily runs, on the agility course, or in the obedience ring. The breed's coat comes in liver and white or black and white and needs only occasional brushing to keep it looking its best.

In addition to hip dysplasia and progressive retinal atrophy, Springers are susceptible to cataracts and glaucoma, as well as disc disease. Also on their list of health concerns are heart disease, epilepsy, and immune-mediated hemolytic anemia. Phosphofructokinase (PFK) deficiency is a genetic disease, causing affected dogs to become weak and lethargic, but, fortunately, there is a test for this condition. Before buying your puppy, make sure that the breeder has tested the parents and hasn't bred two carriers. A Springer's lifespan is between twelve and fourteen years.

Cocker Spaniel

Welsh Springer Spaniel

AMONG THE AKC'S TERRIERS ARE:

- Airedale Terrier
- American Hairless Terrier
- American Staffordshire Terrier
- Border Terrier
- Bull Terrier
- Cesky Terrier
- Dandie Dinmont Terrier
- Irish Terrier
- Kerry Blue Terrier
- Manchester Terrier
- Miniature Bull Terrier
- Miniature Schnauzer
- Norfolk Terrier
- Norwich Terrier
- Parson Russell Terrier
- Russell Terrier
- Scottish Terrier
- Smooth Fox Terrier
- Soft Coated Wheaten Terrier
- Staffordshire Bull Terrier
- West Highland White Terrier
- Wire Fox Terrier

Almost all of the terriers originated in the British Isles, and the majority of terriers has a harsh, wiry outer coat and a softer undercoat, offering good protection against both harsh weather and against the animals they were bred to hunt. The terriers that have short, smooth coats are the American Staffordshire Terrier, Bull Terrier, Manchester Terrier, Miniature Bull Terrier, and Smooth Fox Terrier. The American Hairless Terrier comes in a hairless and a coated variety, and Parson Russell Terriers and Russell Terriers come in smooth and wire coats. Bedlingtons have woolly coats, making them look a bit like lambs,

Bedlington Terrier

and Soft Coated Wheaten Terriers have, as their name suggests, a softer coat.

The name "terrier" comes from the Latin *terra*, meaning "earth," and these dogs were bred to go to ground after rats, mice, fox, and badger. In the United States, they'll happily dig out a woodchuck. Most of these dogs make good watchdogs, and all of them, regardless of size, are fearless. Terriers are intelligent, but they can also have a stubborn streak, and they may not always get along with other dogs or with cats. If you have small pets, like guinea pigs or hamsters, make sure they're in secure housing and the dog can't reach them.

Terriers being groomed for the show ring have their coats stripped, or hand plucked. Pets will need regular grooming appointments. Some people shave their terriers' coats, and this changes the texture considerably. If you're not showing your dog, this isn't a catastrophe, but it does diminish the weatherproof qualities of the coat.

The Miniature Schnauzer is one of the most popular dogs in the Terrier Group. This compact little dog stands between 12 and 14 inches at the shoulder and weighs between 11 and 20 pounds. He loves being with his owners and is very energetic. If you're interested in competitive events, consider this breed; Miniature Schnauzers are great for earthdog trials and agility, among other sports.

Health concerns include progressive retinal atrophy and von Willebrand's disease, so make sure that the puppy's parents have been tested for these conditions. Miniature Schnauzers may also be affected by a condition called urolithiasis, which can cause kidney stones. Your dog may require surgery, and your vet may advise you to put your dog on a special diet to help decrease the chance of stones forming. Congenital megaesophagus is a condition that affects the esophagus. Affected dogs can accidentally inhale food and water into their lungs, which can lead to pneumonia. Comedone syndrome is also known as "Schnauzer bumps," nicknamed after the breed it mainly

affects. These bumps are blackheads and scabs that form on the dogs' back, sometimes leading to hair loss. This condition can be managed with medicated shampoos or wipes. The Miniature Schnauzer's life span is twelve to fourteen years.

West Highland White Terriers are solid, compact dogs weighing between 15 and 22 pounds and standing about 10 inches high at the shoulder. Originally, they were considered the white version of the Scottish Terrier. Westies are energetic and will definitely let their owners know if someone's at the door or if there's a squirrel in the yard. Some health problems include luxating patellas, Legg-Calve-Perthes disease, dry eye, Addison's disease (a disease of the adrenal glands), and idiopathic pulmonary fibrosis (a.k.a.Westie lung disease). In the

Miniature Schnauzer puppy

latter disease, the air sacs and connective tissue in the lungs become inflamed and scarred, which causes progressive breathing problems. The breed's life span is fifteen to twenty years.

Soft Coated Wheaten Terriers are a bit bigger than many of the terriers, standing between 16 and 18 inches at the shoulder and weighing 30 to 40 pounds. They need a bit more grooming and exercise than most other terriers, but like all terriers, they love the chase. Health concerns include hip dysplasia, Addison's disease, and a kidney disease known as renal dysplasia. Two breed-specific problems are protein-losing nephropathy, in which protein is lost through the kidneys; and protein-losing enteropathy, which is a loss of protein from the intestines that may be a symptom of several diseases or conditions.

Bull Terriers are solid, fun-loving, playful dogs weighing 50 to 70 pounds and standing about 22 inches at the shoulder. They may not love other dogs, but they'll love all of your family members and will welcome strangers, too. They have short, easy-care coats and will happily join you in whatever

Miniature Bull Terrier

activity you have in mind. Genetic problems include heart disease, deafness, luxating patellas, dry eye, and ectropion. Entropion causes the lower eyelid to turn outward, exposing the inner eyelid and causing irritation. Bull Terriers are also prone to allergies, causing itching and ear infections. The Bull Terrier's lifespan is ten to twelve years.

Airedale Terriers are the largest terriers, and they were much more popular in the early 1900s than they are today. They were used by the military in World War I. Airedales stand 21 to 23 inches at the shoulder and weigh between 40 and 65 pounds. While they are not always good around other dogs or smaller animals, they are intelligent and loyal. No matter how active you are, the Airedale can keep up, but he needs guidance so that he's not destructive. Health concerns include hip dysplasia, renal disease, hypothyroidism, and dilated cardiomyopathy. The Airedale's life span is ten to thirteen years.

23 Non-Sporting Group

THE AKC'S NON-SPORTING GROUP INCLUDES:

- Bichon Frise
- Boston Terrier
- Bulldog
- Chow Chow
- Dalmatian
- French Bulldog
- Keeshond
- Lhasa Apso
- Lowchen
- Norwegian Lundehund
- Poodle
- Schipperke
- Shiba Inu
- Tibetan Spaniel
- Tibetan Terrier
- Xoloitzcuintli

Many of the dogs in the Non-Sporting Group used to have specific jobs but, for one reason or another, they no longer do those jobs. For example, the Dalmatian used to run alongside horse-drawn coaches to guard them and deter robbers. The Norwegian Lundehund was bred to hunt puffins and has extra toes on each foot to make rock climbing easier. These breeds are now classified in the Non-Sporting Group because they don't seem to fit any of the other groups.

Sizes and energy levels range widely in this group. The Dalmatian is the tallest and arguably the most energetic, although the diminutive Schipperke is pretty high-energy, too. Standard and

Young Schipperke

Miniature Poodles find themselves in this group along with the American Eskimo Dog, which comes in three sizes: the toy measures between 9 and 12 inches, the miniature measures between 12 and 15 inches, and the standard measures between 15 and 19 inches. These dogs are friendly, intelligent, and playful, and they also make good watchdogs. If you don't mind a lot of hair, you might consider an American Eskimo Dog.

Bulldogs consistently rank among the AKC's most popular breeds. They may look gruff and tough, but they are really lovable family companions. They don't need much exercise, so they're a good choice for apartment living. Because of their short noses, they can overheat easily and may suffer from heatstroke; in hot weather, take that walk around the block early in the morning or in the evening when it's cooler. Bulldogs have short coats, so grooming is simple, but those wrinkles need daily care. Some Bulldogs have an elongated palate, which can make breathing even more difficult, and they are prone to eye diseases and subject to bloat.

Toy Poodles are 10 inches and under at the shoulder, while Miniatures are more than 10 but less than 15 inches at the shoulder. Poodles in all three varieties are intelligent, playful pets who can conquer just about any dog sport, from retrieving ducks to obedience and agility to dock diving—and everything in between. Don't be put off by the show clip—you can keep your Poodle in a modified puppy clip. Poodles don't shed, which is part of their popularity, but you will need to visit a groomer every four to six weeks or learn to clip your dog yourself. Health concerns include hip dysplasia, bloat, progressive retinal atrophy, Addison's disease, Cushing's disease, and hypothyroidism. A Poodle's lifespan is fourteen to eighteen years.

French Bulldogs have the Bulldog look in a smaller package, usually less than 28 pounds. Their huge "bat ears" make them irresistible. They don't need much exercise and, like Bulldogs, can succumb to heatstroke, so it's important to keep them from overheating. Also like the Bulldog, Frenchies may have elongated palates and other problems that restrict breathing. They can suffer from spinal malformations as well as intervertebral disc disease. The breed's life span is nine to eleven years.

Don't forget about Boston Terriers! These lively little dogs are love bugs, always willing to cuddle and always up for a game, including agility. Bostons have flat faces, although not as extreme as in Bulldogs and French Bulldogs, and may have some breathing problems (they're known for their snoring). The Boston's corkscrew tail is associated with hemivertebrae, a failure in the development of the spine that may require surgery. Eye problems include cataracts, corneal ulcers, and glaucoma as well as eye injuries due to their flat faces and prominent eyes. The Boston's lifespan is between nine and eleven years.

The Bichon Frise is a charming companion but can be challenging to housetrain. Between 10 and 18 pounds, the Bichon is a nice portable dog, good for apartment living. The breed is happy to play and can easily learn tricks. They're non-shedding, but they need daily grooming and periodic trimming. A Bichon may develop hip dysplasia or Legg-Calve-Perthes disease, a disease of the thighbone, as well as luxating patellas, like many other small dogs. They may also be prone to cataracts. The Bichon enjoys a long life span of around fifteen years or even more.

Boston Terrier

24 Hound Group

AMONG THE AKC'S HOUND BREEDS ARE:

- Afghan Hound
- American Foxhound
- Basenji
- Basset Hound
- Beagle
- Black and Tan Coonhound
- Bloodhound
- Bluetick Coonhound
- Borzoi
- Cirneco Dell'Etna
- Dachshund
- English Foxhound
- Greyhound
- Irish Wolfhound
- Petit Basset Griffon Vendeen
- Pharaoh Hound
- Redbone Coonhound
- Rhodesian Ridgeback
- Saluki
- Scottish Deerhound
- Treeing Walker Coonhound
- Whippet

The Hound Group is further broken down into two groups into which most hounds fall: those that hunt by sight (sighthounds) and those that hunt by scent (scenthounds). Sighthounds include the Afghan Hound, Basenji, Greyhound, Ibizan Hound, Irish Wolfhound, Rhodesian Ridgeback, Saluki, Scottish Deerhound, and Whippet. In the scenthound category are, among others, the American Foxhound, Basset Hound, Beagle, Black and Tan Coonhound, Bloodhound, Dachshund, Petit Basset Griffon Vendeen, Plott, and Treeing Walker Coonhound. Of course, no dog is going to hunt by sight or scent to the exclusion of other senses; the sighthound or scenthound designation refers to the primary sense used while hunting.

Sighthounds are typically lean and leggy and are able to run rapidly and turn sharply, keeping their prey in sight and, in many cases, running it down. They tend to be silent runners. Scenthounds are generally built closer to the ground and have floppy ears that help funnel scent to their noses. Because moisture helps retain scent, many scenthounds may also have a tendency to drool. Because these dogs may be following trails into brush and out of sight, many of them have loud, insistent voices to enable the hunters to find them.

Both sighthounds and scenthounds can become so focused on their prey that they become oblivious to anything around them. It's easy for them to become lost and also to run out into

The Borzoi is a sighthound.

traffic, barely noticing the cars. A fenced yard is a necessity to keep them safe; in absence of a fenced yard, they need to be kept on leash for walks. In many cases, a loose hound is a lost hound.

Many hounds are hunted in packs and were developed to get along well with other dogs. They are also generally good around people. Some may be a bit aloof, but they are rarely aggressive toward people. The sighthounds don't make good watchdogs, but the scenthounds have good, deep barks and will probably warn you of any stranger approaching.

With the exception of the Afghan Hound, none of the dogs in this group requires much in the way of grooming. You can do any brushing or bathing yourself, without the help of a professional groomer. If you decide on an Afghan Hound and are not planning to show the dog, you can opt for a puppy clip, which is easier to maintain than the long, flowing coat of a show dog.

NORWEGIAN ELKHOUND

Many feel that the Norwegian Elkhound should be classified in either the Sporting or the Working Group. It ended up with the hounds because the word "hound" is in its name. As the breed's name suggests, it was used in Norway to hunt elk.

It's always dangerous to make blanket statements, but if you're looking for a dog to compete in obedience or agility, you should probably look in a different group. I have known people to successfully put obedience titles on Basenjis and Greyhounds, but this is not typical. If you're looking forward to playing fetch with your dog, this is also the wrong group. These dogs were not bred to bring things back. That's not to say they won't play, but they're not as driven to play as, say, a Golden Retriever. On the other hand, many of the dogs in this group would make excellent jogging companions.

The Beagle is the most popular breed in the Hound Group, and they come in two varieties: the 13-inch and the 15-inch. They have happy dispositions and are content with moderate exercise, especially if it includes following scents wherever Beagles lead. Both sizes are nice and compact as well. Reputable breeders will test dogs for hip dysplasia, and other concerns in the breed include hypothyroidism, diabetes, cataracts, and allergies. Beagles have a life span of thirteen to sixteen years.

Dachshunds also come in two sizes, miniature (11 pounds and under) and standard (16 to 32 pounds), as well as three coat types, smooth, longhaired, and wirehaired. They are fearless and determined dogs who will bark an alarm at just about anything. They may not be the best choice for families with small children because of the dog's short stature and long backs. You must be careful when picking up a Dachshund and be aware that they are prone to back problems; don't let them jump off chairs or beds. Consider ramps if you want your Dachshund to share the couch with you. Health concerns in the breed, besides back injuries, include bloat, diabetes, and progressive retinal atrophy. The average life span is twelve to fifteen years.

Basset Hounds are slow-moving, gentle dogs who make loving pets and live to follow their noses. Like Dachshunds, Bassets have long backs, which makes jumping down from chairs and sofas a bad idea. You may think of the breed as small because Bassets are low to the ground, but an adult Basset weighs between 50 and 65 pounds. They've got a good, deep voice.

Basset Hound breeding stock should be tested for both thrombopathia and von Willebrand's disease, both bleeding disorders. Bassets are also prone to hypothyroidism, elbow dysplasia, and skin infections. They have a life expectancy of between twelve and fifteen years.

Most Bloodhound owners will tell you that their dogs live to eat, sleep, and trail.

The Bloodhound is a scenthound.

They also drool a lot. They are gentle dogs, weighing between 80 and 110 pounds. While they love to be with people, they can be stubborn, and they aren't interested in playing typical dog games, such as fetch. If you want to train a search and rescue dog, this breed, with its superior nose, is one of the best. Health concerns include hip and elbow dysplasia, hypothryoidism, dry eye, and bloat. The Bloodhound's life expectancy is eight to ten years.

Whippets are graceful sighthounds with short, easy-to-care-for coats. They were bred to chase and kill vermin and small game, so if you've got rabbits or small rodents as pets, keep them far out of your Whippet's reach. Whippets need warm coats for protection outdoors if you live somewhere with a lot of rain or snow. Health concerns include corneal dystrophy, progressive retinal atrophy, hypothyriodism, and congenital deafness. It's also important to know that because of their low percentage of body fat, sighthounds, the Whippet included, may be ultra-sensitive to anesthetics. The breed's life span is twelve to fifteen years.

The breeds in the Miscellaneous Class are seeking full AKC recognition and are shown at conformation shows in the Miscellaneous Class, but they can't win points toward a championship. They may also compete in performance events.

To become eligible for inclusion in the Miscellaneous Class, the breed's parent club must submit a written request to the AKC. The AKC then considers if the breed has met the following requirements (from www.akc.org):

- A demonstrated following and interest (minimum of 100 active household members) in the breed (in the form of a National Breed Club).
- A sufficient population in this country (minimum of 300-400 dogs) with a three-generation pedigree. Dogs in that pedigree must all be of the same breed.
- Geographic distribution of the dogs and people (located in twenty or more states).
- AKC must review and approve the club's breed standard as well as the club's constitution and by-laws. Breed observations must be completed by AKC Field Staff.

If the breed meets these criteria, the AKC's Board of Directors then considers its acceptance into the Miscellaneous Class. Once a breed becomes a Miscellaneous Class member, the breed club is required to prepare and provide the AKC with certain

Azawakh

annual statistics, including how many dogs and litters have been recorded and how many dogs have competed in AKC events. In addition, the club must hold matches, breed specialty shows (shows in which only their breed is permitted), and breed-education workshops and seminars. Breeds often remain in the Miscellaneous Class for several years until the Board of Directors allows them to become fully recognized, at which point they are moved into one of the aforementioned seven regular groups.

26 Alternative Registration

If you buy a purebred puppy from a breeder, she will give you the necessary paperwork to register your dog with the American Kennel Club (AKC) or the United Kennel Club (UKC), but what if you get a purebred without "papers" or a mixed-breed and want to compete in performance events? Both the AKC and the UKC make that possible.

The AKC offers the Purebred Alternative Listing/Indefinite Listing Privilege (PAL/ILP) for purebreds without papers. To apply for this type of registration, you'll need to supply photos to prove that your dog is one of the breeds recognized by the AKC, and your dog must be spayed or neutered. For all of the details, check out the "Owners" section at www.akc.org.

If you have a mixed-breed or a breed not recognized by the AKC, you can enroll in the AKC Canine Partners Program to be eligible to compete in certain performance events. Again, the dog must be spayed or neutered. For more information, click on the "Owners" section of the AKC's website.

The UKC offers a similar program, called Performance Listing, whereby mixed-breed dogs, purebred dogs with no registration papers, or breeds not recognized by the UKC can register to participate in performance events. In addition to being able to compete in UKC performance events, Performance-Listed dogs may compete in Junior Showmanship events.

Go to the UKC website (www.ukcdogs.com) for the Performance Listing application. As with the AKC program, you will need to supply two photos of your dog, one full front view and one side view, with the dog standing.

If you live near the Canadian border, you may want to show your dog in Canada; if you have an AKC-registered dog, the Canadian Kennel Club (CKC) makes that possible. Your dog must be a CKC-recognized breed and have a microchip or tattoo. Along with your application for registration, you must include a copy of the AKC registration certificate and a copy of your dog's certified pedigree for at least three generations (you can get a certified pedigree from the AKC).

If you have a mixed breed or a breed not recognized by the CKC, you can get a Canine Companion number and compete in specific performance events. The dog must be spayed or neutered and must have a CKC-approved microchip. For all of the details, check out the Events tab on the CKC's website (www. ckc.ca).

If your dog of choice is a Border Collie, it may be registered with the American Border Collie Association (ABCA). The ABCA registers, maintains, and verifies the pedigrees of Border Collies and also promotes stockdog trials and exhibitions. Not all Border Collie fanciers were in favor of the AKC acceptance of their breed, so you may find a breeder who prefers to register with the ABCA rather than the AKC. Visit the ABCA online at www. americanbordercollie.org.

The National Greyhound Association (NGA) is the recognized registry for racing Greyhounds in North America. If you have adopted a retired racing Greyhound, you can register him with the NGA. After you pay the registration fee, you will receive a registration certificate that lists all of your adopted dog's information, including the dog's official NGA name, color, sex, date of birth, and two-generation pedigree. The NGA will then donate part of your registration fee to the Greyhound pet adoption group of your choice, which will help find homes for other retired racing Greyhounds. Visit the NGA at www.ngagreyhounds.com.

Greyhounds

27 New-Dog Checklist

What will come home with your dog depends on where you get your dog. If your dog is coming from a shelter, you may get a spay/neuter certificate and proof of a rabies vaccination—and that's it. If your dog is from a rescue organization, he may have been staying in a foster home, so he may come with a leash and collar, a toy, and even a bed along with his vaccination records and spay/neuter certificate. It is likely that the foster volunteer will give you some of the food that the dog is used to. You may also get a report on the dog's likes and dislikes and behavior in certain situations, such as around children or other animals.

If you are buying from a breeder, you should expect registration papers, vaccination records, copies of health-testing results, and a copy of the contract between you and the breeder. This contract will spell out exactly what you and the breeder have agreed to. This document will list the price of the puppy and whether the puppy may be returned to the breeder; if so, the contract will state if there is a time limit and if you will receive a refund. Many breeders will offer a refund or another puppy if the puppy is examined by a veterinarian within forty-eight hours of purchase and is found to have a genetic condition or a serious disease. Furthermore, most reputable breeders will agree to take the dog back at any time during the dog's life for any reason but will not offer a replacement or refund after a specified period of time. If you've entered into a co-ownership arrangement, the contract will include its conditions.

Some breeders send puppies home with a crate, a collar and leash, or a special toy, and many breeders will include a book on the breed or on general puppy care. The most important thing you can get from a breeder, in addition to the puppy, is her phone number. Responsible breeders want their puppies to go to good homes, and they want to help you with any problems or issues. If you're a first-time owner, it's reassuring to know that the breeder will be there for you with support and advice.

At a minimum, you'll need dishes for food and water, a collar or harness and a leash, food, and some kind of a bed. If your dog has no proof of any vaccinations, you'll need to make an appointment with a veterinarian immediately; even if your dog is up to date on shots, a checkup by your vet is still a good idea.

Your Dog and Your Bathroom

Once you have a dog, you will never again be alone in the bathroom. Really. Well, OK, if you shut the door firmly and lock it, you'll be fine—but if not, be prepared for a canine invasion. If you're not used to it, it may be a little disconcerting in the beginning.

This joke has been around the Internet for a while and pretty much lays it out: "For the last time, there is not a secret exit from the bathroom. If, by some miracle, I beat you there and manage to get the door shut, it is not necessary to claw, whine, try to turn the knob, or get your paw under the edge and try to pull the door open. I must exit through the same door I entered. In addition, I have been using bathrooms for years. Canine attendance is not mandatory."

I don't know about other breeds, but this certainly describes my Corgis and their behavior when anyone manages to escape their watchful eye and make it into the bathroom unescorted. When my husband would shut the bathroom door to shower, Griffin used to whine piteously outside in the hall. It was pathetic. He would lie with his nose to the crack in the door, and nothing could convince him that Jim was safe. Griffin was convinced that Jim was drowning. I called it his "Timmy down the well" act. His joy when the door opened and he discovered that Jim was alive was amazing. On occasion, he managed to push the door open while Jim was still in the shower. Then he would lie down in the bathroom, facing the shower. If he could, I'm sure he would have grabbed Jim by the ankle and rescued him from the flood.

I never evoked the same reaction. When I showered, Griffin didn't seem to care one way or another. I never knew whether to be relieved or annoyed. It was nice to be able to dry off without a dog licking my toes, but what did this mean in terms of our relationship? Was I not worth saving, or did Griffin just think I was a better swimmer than my husband?

There's no answer to any of this. Maybe you'll have a dog who's content to leave you alone in the bathroom, but don't count on it.

Your New Dog's Health

Before your dog comes home, think about what kind of veterinary care you'll want. Yes, you can find a veterinarian after you've gotten your dog, but it really is better to choose a vet first. You should take your dog in for a checkup as soon as you get him. If you're getting a purebred from a breeder, there will be a short window of time, usually 48 hours, during which the breeder will take the puppy back and refund you the purchase price if there's a health problem. If you are getting a dog from a shelter, there may not be a return policy, but you'll still want to know right away if your new pal has any health issues. When caught early, a problem may be easily treatable.

Don't just flip through the Yellow Pages and choose the first veterinarian listed or the one closest to where you live. What do you want in veterinary care? If you've chosen a breed that has specific health problems, find a vet who understands that breed. Bulldogs, as an example, may have breathing problems or reproductive issues, and you'll want a vet who has experience with the breed.

Consider distance. A veterinarian 30 miles away may come highly recommended, and you may not mind the drive for routine visits, but what happens in an emergency? You may want to find a veterinarian who is a bit closer or at least find a nearby emergency veterinary clinic.

How many doctors are in the practice? If you go to a practice with just one doctor, that doctor will get to know you and your dog, and you will form a rapport with him or her. In a practice with multiple doctors, you may not have the individual rapport with one doctor, but all of the doctors will have access to your dog's medical records. Another benefit to a practice with multiple doctors may be in the way that they handle emergencies. With several doctors, someone is most likely "on call" at night and on weekends. If you choose a practice with just one veterinarian, ask how the vet handles emergencies. Does another practice cover for him or her, or is there an emergency veterinary clinic in your area? Ask these questions now so that you're not wasting critical time trying to find a vet if you have an emergency with your dog.

If possible, visit the office before you make your decision. The waiting room should be clean, and the staff should be friendly. Separate areas for cats and dogs are a plus, but not a must.

You may need to make that initial appointment before you can come to a final decision on the best vet for you and your dog. If everything about the clinic meets your approval, but you just don't feel comfortable with a particular vet, find another one. You and your vet will be partners in keeping your dog healthy. You need to feel comfortable asking questions, and you need to have confidence that your vet is giving your dog the best care possible.

The same goes for the staff. While you might not be able to get a feel for the staff with just one visit, remember that you'll typically be dealing with the staff as much as you're dealing with the doctor. Does the staff treat you—and your dog—with consideration? Do they take your concerns seriously? In a true emergency, I want to know that the staff will make every effort to get my dog the attention she needs.

Here's an example from my own experience. Years ago, we moved to a new

WAITING ROOM TIP
If your dog is uncomfortable in the waiting room, whether from nerves due to being at the veterinarian's office or because of the other animals, wait with him outside until you're called into the exam room.

area. One of my dogs had broken a nail so that it stuck out at a right angle. It wasn't life-threatening, but he was in pain, and it was difficult for him to walk. I called a veterinary hospital not far from our home and was told that someone could see me in five days. I called another practice that was a bit farther away, and they told me to bring the dog in immediately. Guess which practice has had my business for more than twenty years?

Another consideration is the specific kind of medicine you may want available to your dog, like acupuncture or chiropractic treatments. Maybe you're more comfortable with a vet who uses a traditional approach, or maybe you like the idea of a holistic vet. Find out what the practice offers. Maybe the clinic doesn't offer chiropractic treatments but can refer you to a chiropractor who will work on your dog.

This section of the book discusses some different types of care or treatment that you might want to consider. Some are more traditional and some are more holistic. It's up to you and your vet to determine just what kind of care you want for your dog.

Technically, the term "neutering" applies to both castrating a male (removing the testicles) and spaying a female (removing the ovaries or both the ovaries and the uterus), but "neutering" has come to refer to males and "spaying" to females. Regardless of what you call it, if you don't plan to breed or show your dog, then spaying and neutering can be a good idea. First and foremost, it prevents unwanted litters that frequently end up in shelters or are otherwise disposed of.

An intact male can detect a female in heat and will then have his mind on only one thing: getting to that female. He will try to escape from your yard and can make walks miserable by pulling and tugging in the direction of the female. He will likely "mark" more than usual, sprinkling areas indoors and out with urine.

Intact males are more likely to mark territory, especially when he detects a female in heat.

Females in heat may be cranky and, depending on the dog, she may create more mess when she comes into season every six months or so than you want to deal with. You'll need to keep a close watch on a female in season, and, if you have an intact male in your household as well, it is best to separate them or maybe even board one or the other.

In males, neutering prevents problems such as prostate cancer and testicular tumors. Neutering may also make a dog less aggressive, and a neutered male may be less likely to urine-mark areas inside your home.

With females, spaying decreases the chances of cancerous mammary tumors and eliminates any chance of pyometra, a life-threatening infection of the uterus. It generally occurs in older dogs, but it can occur any time, and the symptoms are not always easy to spot. If not treated, pyometra will kill the dog.

Traditionally, the rule was to spay or neuter at six months of age, but then it was determined that animals can be spayed or neutered as young as six to eight weeks old. This was good news for shelters as well as for breeders who wanted to make sure that dogs with genetic defects or major faults were not bred. However, having the procedure done at such a young age is not always the best idea because it may negatively affect the size, shape, and structure of the dog. It may lead to urinary incontinence in both sexes. Beyond that, there can be even more serious effects.

According to an article by Demian Dressler, DVM (www.dogcancerblog.com), if a male Rottweiler is neutered before one year of age, the risk of osteosarcoma almost quadruples. In a female Rottweiler spayed before one year of age, the risk more than triples. In any purebred dog spayed or neutered before one year of age, the osteosarcoma risk more than doubles.

A study at the University of California, Davis, showed that male Golden Retrievers neutered before one year of age have an increased incidence of hip dysplasia, torn cruciate ligaments, and lymphosarcoma. Labrador Retrievers neutered before six months of age have an increased incidence of hip dysplasia, torn cruciate ligaments, and elbow dysplasia.

In a January 2012 article in *Veterinary Practice News*, Alice Villalobos, DVM, cites a study by Christine Zink, DVM, that suggests that dogs neutered early (before five and a half months old) have a higher incidence of orthopedic disease. She notes that a 1999 study by Ware *et al.* found a five-times greater risk of cardiac hemangiosarcoma in spayed versus intact female dogs and an almost two-and-a-half times greater risk of that disease in neutered dogs versus intact males.

The larger the breed, the more I'd be inclined not to spay or neuter until the dog was at least a year old, but this is an issue you need to discuss with your veterinarian. Weigh the risks and advantages of spaying and neutering with a veterinary professional before you make a decision.

Female and male Rottweilers

Female Chinese Crested

Although many veterinarians follow traditional medical practices, many also recognize the value of alternative treatments and use them in addition to traditional practices to help pets heal faster or to help them cope with pain or the side effects of medicines. The following may be methods you'll want to consider in your search for veterinary care.

Acupuncture

Acupuncture

You don't have to be afraid of these needles, and your dog won't mind them at all. Acupuncture needles are hair-fine needles used to stimulate certain points on the body. These points are areas that contain concentrated levels of nerve endings and blood vessels. Acupuncture has been used on people for more than 4,500 years and on animals for at least 2,000 years. Studies have shown that acupuncture increases blood flow, which speeds healing. Acupuncture lowers heart rate and can improve immune-system function. It also encourages the release of the body's natural painkillers as well as cortisol, an anti-inflammatory steroid produced by the body.

Acupuncture is used to treat such conditions as arthritis, allergies, and skin conditions. It may also help with epilepsy, and it may ease the side effects of cancer treatment. A veterinarian may make a diagnosis using traditional methods and then use or recommend acupuncture to help ease pain and hasten healing. Ask your veterinarian about acupuncturists in your area or search for veterinary acupuncturists by state at the International Veterinary Acupuncture Society's website: www.ivas.org.

Holistic Treatment

Holistic veterinary medicine deals with the whole dog, not just individual parts. Holistic practitioners study the entire animal, including the physical and social environment, not just the symptoms, and the holistic vet may recommend a combination of methods for treatment. Holistic treatment techniques include acupuncture, chiropractic adjustments, dietary changes, herbs, massage, and Reiki (Reiki produces results similar to acupuncture but without the needles). Your veterinarian may use any or all of these methods or, depending on your area, may send you to someone who specializes in one of these techniques.

Chiropractic

Chiropractic adjustments manipulate the spine and connecting bones. The theory is that if the bones are out of alignment, nerves are irritated and will cause discomfort. Chiropractors realign the bones. Dogs who are very active or who compete in strenuous events, such as agility, may need occasional adjustments. Before you visit a chiropractor for your dog, make sure that your vet has first examined him to rule out other causes of his lameness or soreness, such as a tumor. To find an animal chiropractor, check the website of the American Veterinary Chiropractic Association at www.animalchiropractic.org.

Herbs and Flowers

TCM stands for Traditional Chinese Medicine, a type of treatment that uses herbs and herbal compounds in treating a pet. Used correctly, these may be gentler on an animal's system than a synthetic compound but get the same results. When used as prescribed by a veterinarian, herbs may help your dog, but don't attempt to concoct your own herbal remedy unless you are trained in their use. Just because something is "natural" doesn't mean that it's safe. There are many deadly poisons that are "natural."

If you research herb and flower uses, you will discover Bach flower essences, named after Edward Bach who, in the 1800s, studied the healing properties of plants. Many people swear by Bach's Rescue Remedy, which is used in cases of shock, collapse, or trauma. There is a Rescue Remedy formula made for pets, and it is used as a stress reliever for animals in fearful situations, such as during thunderstorms or fireworks displays.

Massage

Massage is not a medical treatment, but it can help relax your dog and can also ease sore muscles. The best-known massage technique is Tellington TTouch, developed by Linda Tellington-Jones. This method uses repeated massage strokes to help ease anxiety, and the calming effect can help promote healing.

Massaging your dog at the end of a long day can be soothing to both you and your dog. Not all dogs love massage, and the object is to soothe, not annoy. Also, no massage technique is a substitute for veterinary care. If your dog is limping or in pain, it's time to visit your vet.

Depending on where you get your dog and how old the dog is, he may need to get certain shots. Typically, puppies get shots at eight, twelve, and sixteen weeks, and then annually after that. These shots will inoculate your pet against distemper, hepatitis, parainfluenza, and parvovirus; he may also get a vaccine for leptospirosis. The rabies shot is the one vaccine that is required by law in every state. In some states, your dog must get a rabies shot every year; in others, it's every three years. Whether you get a puppy or an adult dog, be sure to also get his vaccination record so you will know what he has and what he still needs. An adult dog with an unknown vaccination schedule will likely follow the same schedule as a puppy.

It used to be the norm for a dog to get all of his shots, including rabies, in one office visit. Now, veterinarians are moving away from that practice and are breaking up the shots into multiple visits. Your dog may receive the rabies shot during one visit and then distemper and parvovirus in another. Some vets don't even recommend the leptospirosis vaccine because it seems to be the one that most often causes adverse reactions in dogs.

Talk to your veterinarian about vaccines and which ones he or she recommends and how often. If you and your dog participate in dog sports, your dog may

have a different vaccination schedule than a dog who never leaves his property.

The first time your dog gets shots, stay in the vet's waiting room for a while afterward to see whether or not the dog has a reaction. A mild reaction might be some swelling at the site of the injection. Or, your dog could itch or get hives. His face might swell, or he might vomit or have diarrhea. If you've already gone home before any symptoms have shown themselves, call your veterinarian immediately.

My younger Corgi reacts to something in the distemper/hepatitis/parvovirus vaccine, and her face gets puffy. So far, it has never interfered with her breathing, but I always watch her closely. Her reaction may never get worse, or it could get much worse rapidly. Before we go for the shot, I give her Benadryl, and I monitor her closely for several hours afterward.

Vaccination helps prevent the spread of disease from dog to dog.

Following are the most common diseases that you are likely to have your dog vaccinated against.

Rabies is the one vaccine your dog absolutely must have. In addition to being required by law, it is the only protection your dog has against this fatal and dangerous disease. The rabies virus attacks the central nervous system and is spread through the saliva of an infected animal. Common carriers include bats, foxes, raccoons, and skunks.

The distemper shot is not required, but distemper is another deadly virus. Distemper is highly contagious and has a very low recovery rate. The threat is greatest for dogs younger than six months and older than six years, and symptoms include coughing, vomiting, and fever.

Parvovirus is another nasty virus that is potentially fatal. While an adult dog with a mild case may recover, puppies are highly susceptible and generally die. No matter what the dog's age, if there is vomiting and bloody diarrhea, the outlook is not good. Other symptoms include fever, lethargy, and depression.

Leptospirosis bacteria are generally transmitted through the urine of rats and mice and can cause renal failure. If there is a chance that your dog will be exposed to rats and mice, get him the leptospirosis shot; otherwise, you may want to skip this shot because the leptospirosis vaccine in combination with other vaccines seems to increase the risk of a reaction. There is, however, a newer leptospirosis vaccine that causes a milder reaction and can be given as a separate shot; talk to your veterinarian about this.

Hepatitis spreads through the feces and urine of dogs, and, although a dog will usually recover in about a week from a mild to moderate case, severe cases can cause death. Your dog may have a fever and be reluctant to move. His abdomen may be tender and his mucus membranes may turn pale. In severe cases, there may be vomiting, diarrhea, and a cough.

Lyme disease causes lethargy, lameness, and loss of appetite. If caught early, it can be treated with antibiotics, but if undiagnosed, it can continue to flare up throughout the dog's life. Deer ticks spread Lyme disease, which is more prevalent in the eastern and northeastern parts of the country. Talk to your veterinarian about whether this vaccine is essential for your dog.

There are tick preventatives on the market; discuss their safety and efficacy with your veterinarian. Given how many diseases ticks can carry and their increasing prevalence, a preventative can be a good idea in addition to the Lyme vaccine.

Bordetella, also known as "kennel cough," is a highly contagious airborne disease. Most boarding kennels and doggy daycares require this vaccination before they will accept your dog, even though there are more than 100 strains of *Bordetella* and the vaccine only protects against a few of them. If your dog has a dry, hacking cough and has been around other dogs, he may have kennel cough. While no disease should be taken lightly, kennel cough can be treated with antibiotics and is not usually serious.

33 General Health Concerns

Don't let health concerns prevent you from getting a dog. It can be scary and a little intimidating when you're researching a breed to see a long list of ailments that the breed may be susceptible to, but think of all the diseases that humans can get. Many are curable or have symptoms that can be managed with medicine. Many are not life-threatening, and a person will not experience most of them in his or her lifetime. It's the same with dogs.

PET INSURANCE

Animal medicine is advancing as fast as its human counterpart, with MRIs, hip replacements, and cancer treatments that include surgery, chemotherapy, and radiation. All of these treatments are expensive, and you may want to consider pet insurance to help out with veterinary costs.

There are many different types of pet insurance policies. Some cover annual checkups but may not cover hereditary conditions or specialists. Some may not cover alternative therapies, like acupuncture. Some will cover accidents, injuries, or illnesses but not annual checkups. Do your research before selecting a policy.

Mixed-breed adult

Knowing what diseases your chosen dog may be prone to will help you to recognize the symptoms if they should appear, allowing you to get help sooner. Also, you'll know what health checks your breeder should have done on the parents of your prospective pup. As an example, any dog can have hip dysplasia, but it's more prevalent in larger breeds. I might consider getting a Corgi puppy from a breeder who did not check the parents for hip dysplasia, but I would not get that puppy if the parents hadn't been tested for either progressive retinal atrophy or von Willebrand's disease.

Health problems don't affect just purebred dogs. If you're getting a mixed breed, you never know what he may have inherited from his parents. My St. Bernard/German Shepherd Dog cross had one of the worst cases I ever saw of hip dysplasia in a medium-sized mix. Yes, there is such a thing as hybrid vigor, but it's most prevalent in the offspring of two different purebred dogs. If you fall for a puppy whose parents were both mixed breeds, you're just as likely to face health concerns as someone with a purebred.

Do your research. Know what you might be up against, whether with a purebred or, if you know the mix, a mixed breed. Perform health checks, if applicable. Schedule annual visits with your veterinarian and discuss vaccines and preventatives, like those for heartworm. Feed a quality food. And then relax. With time and observation, you'll be able to tell if that limp is just the result of a hard day at play or something more serious. You'll know if you need to get your dog to the vet for digestive issues or if a couple of days on a bland diet will fix things. Enjoy your dog. Don't let fear of a disease rob you of the joy of a canine companion.

HEALTH CHECKS

Remember, health checks are not guarantees that your dog will never have a health problem, but they're a good first step to ensuring that your dog will have a long, healthy life.

Cardigan Welsh Corgi

Dogs of all sizes can suffer from orthopedic injuries. Following are some of the most common.

Anterior Cruciate Ligament (ACL) Tears

According to an article at www.canineortho. com, ACL tears make up more than 65% of all canine orthopedic surgery. Any dog can tear an ACL, sometimes by just jumping off the couch. Furthermore, almost all dogs with knee arthritis have ACL tears. Dogs with ACL tears may limp and sit sideways on one hip instead of sitting straight up. Surgery is necessary to avoid osteoarthritis. Recovery time after the surgery takes about twelve weeks, but once he has healed, there are no restrictions on what the dog can do.

Elbow Dysplasia

Elbow dysplasia involves multiple developmental abnormalities of the dog's elbow joint, especially in the growth of cartilage. One cause of elbow dysplasia is osteochondritis dissecans, which is the separation of a flap of cartilage from the elbow joint's surface. As with hip dysplasia, larger dogs are at a greater risk of this problem. Diet and exercise may ease a dog's pain, but an affected dog may need surgery.

Hip Dysplasia

Hip dysplasia is a malformation of the socket of the hip joint. The socket wears on the head of the femur, and it then doesn't fit properly into the joint. Sometimes it even comes out of the joint altogether, causing pain and

Mastiff

Shetland Sheepdog

ligament damage. Arthritis may also develop in the joint. In some cases, exercise and diet can help, but severe cases need corrective surgery. While larger dogs are more prone to hip dysplasia, it can affect dogs of any size. Reputable breeders will x-ray the hips of their breeding stock, have those x-rays rated by either the Orthopedic Foundation for Animals (OFA; www.ofa.org) or the University of Pennsylvania Hip Improvement Program (PennHIP; www.pennhip.org), and breed only dogs with nondysplastic hips to give the puppies better odds that they will not develop hip dysplasia.

Legg-Calve-Perthes Disease

This condition is seen in small dogs, including the Bichon Frise, Boston Terrier, Chihuahua, Cocker Spaniel, Dachshund, Shetland Sheepdog, Toy Poodle, and Yorkshire Terrier. In this disease, the head of the femur dies and then reforms, causing an irregular fit in the hip socket. This causes stiffness and pain, similar to symptoms of hip dysplasia. The disease appears to be genetic, so dogs with Legg-Calve-Perthes should not be bred.

Patellar Luxation

Patellar luxation is the dislocation of the kneecap. It is found most frequently in very small and very large dogs. The patella, or kneecap, is held in place by ligaments, and it slides in a groove as the joint moves. Sometimes it dislocates, or luxates. If your dog limps, or if his hocks point outward while his toes point inward, the problem may be patellar luxation. Surgery can correct the problem.

Chihuahua and Great Dane

35 Eye Problems

There are a multitude of eye problems and diseases that can affect dogs. Some are breed-specific, some affect older dogs, and others can affect any dog at any time.

Cataracts can be found in any dog at any age. Among purebreds, cataracts are more commonly found in Bichon Frise, Boston Terriers, Cocker Spaniels, Havanese, Miniature Schnauzers, Miniature and Standard Poodles, Silky Terriers, and Smooth Fox Terriers. Diabetic dogs are also prone to cataracts. Surgery is the only option. Untreated cataracts may slip free and can block fluid drainage, which in turn can lead to glaucoma and blindness.

Cherry eye is a red lump in the inner corner of a dog's eye, caused by a prolapse in the tear gland of the third eyelid, which interrupts the blood supply to the gland and dries it out with exposure to air. While any dog can get cherry eye, the breeds more prone to the condition include Beagles, Boston Terriers, Bulldogs, Chinese Shar Peis, and Cocker Spaniels. It's not usually painful, but it does interfere with normal tear production. If the condition is treated by removing the gland, the dog may experience dry eye as he ages. Newer surgical techniques make it possible to save the gland, which is better for the dog's eye.

Collie eye anomaly is an inherited disease that can range from mild, with no vision impairment, to total blindness. It's common in both Rough and Smooth Collies, as the name

Smooth Fox Terrier

Bulldog with cherry eye.

implies, as well as in Australian Shepherds, Bearded Collies, Border Collies, Boykin Spaniels, Lancashire Heelers, Miniature American Shepherds, Nova Scotia Duck Tolling Retrievers, and Shetland Sheepdogs.

Because the disease is so prevalent in Collies, totally eliminating affected dogs—or even carriers—from the gene pool would severely restrict the breed. However, a genetic test developed at Cornell University can determine whether a dog is affected, a carrier, or clear. Since the gene is recessive, this can help breeders limit the transmission of the disease. OptiGen administers the test.

Ectropion is when the eyelids turn outward, exposing the inner lid, which may lead to chronic conjunctivitis or corneal damage. Breeds that commonly experience ectropion include Basset Hounds, Bloodhounds, Clumber Spaniels, Cocker Spaniels, and St. Bernards. The eyelids may be left alone if the condition is not causing any problems, or ectropion can be surgically corrected.

Entropion is the reverse of ectropion. The eyelids turn inward, and the lashes scratch the cornea. This is painful but can be corrected with surgery. It can be hereditary in many breeds, including the Akita, Boxer, Bullmastiff, Chow Chow, Cocker Spaniel, English Springer Spaniel, Labrador Retriever, Pug, Shar Pei, St. Bernard, Welsh Springer Spaniel, and others.

Optic nerve hypoplasia is a hereditary condition in Miniature and Toy Poodles in which the optic nerve fails to develop normally, resulting in blindness. There is no cure, but scientists are working to isolate the gene responsible.

Progressive retinal atrophy (PRA) can be found in many breeds, including, but not limited to, Alaskan Malamutes, Akitas, Corgis (both Cardigan and Pembroke), Irish Setters, Miniature Schnauzers, Papillons, and Samoyeds. PRA affects the rods and cones in the retina and eventually causes blindness. Loss of vision usually begins with night blindness. There is no cure, but breeding stock can be tested through OptiGen, the Orthopedic Foundation for Animals (OFA), or the Canine Eye Registration Foundation.

36 Allergies

Dogs can be allergic to things just as people can, and the causes can be the same, too. Dogs can be allergic to specific foods, molds, pollen, dust, and insect bites. Generally, symptoms in dogs are similar to human reactions to allergens and can include itchy skin, rashes, runny eyes, itchy ears, sneezing, snoring, paw chewing, and constant licking. A food allergy may cause diarrhea.

Veterinarians can perform skin tests and/or skin scrapings on dogs to determine the cause(s) of an allergy. The location of the reaction can also supply a clue as to what the dog is allergic to. For instance, itching on the back and at the base of the tail may be a symptom of a flea-bite allergy. Using a flea preventative may be the answer to this problem. If a dog is biting or chewing at his feet, it could point to a food allergy.

If your dog has a food allergy, it can be very hard to pinpoint the specific foods that are causing the problems. The vet will often recommend putting the dog on a one-ingredient food that he has never had before and then gradually adding ingredients, one at a time, until you discover which ingredient causes the allergic reaction. Or, the veterinarian may recommend that you cook for your dog, in which case you must follow instructions precisely. It can take a while to determine the allergen.

Years ago, one of my Corgis had a food allergy, which I decided was probably corn. I switched to a food without corn and,

NO SMOKING
Dogs may develop bronchitis as an allergic reaction to secondhand smoke. The best cure for that is to not smoke around your dog.

sure enough, the problem disappeared. Years later, he was put on a prescription food that was predominately corn, and he was fine. Obviously, he hadn't been allergic to corn previously, but to another ingredient in the original food that wasn't in the replacement food. The replacement food solved the problem, so it didn't matter that I didn't know the exact cause of the allergy.

In some cases of allergic reactions, such as an ear infection or an insect sting, the symptoms must be treated first. If something stings or bites your dog, and his face begins to swell, he may need an antihistamine shot before the swelling interferes with his breathing.

If your dog seems to have a seasonal allergy to a particular pollen, try to limit your dog's time outdoors. It may also help to give frequent baths to wash pollen out of the fur. With any allergy that causes itching, a bath with medicated shampoo may also help relieve the itching; with a flea-bite allergy, a bath may secondarily kill any fleas on your dog.

Another problem that may result from an allergy but turns into a problem in itself is lick granulomas. Lick granulomas are sores, generally on the paws, caused by incessant licking. A dog may be constantly licking because of an allergy, creating the beginning of a granuloma. Then, the granuloma itself may itch or hurt, causing the dog to lick and nibble even more, increasing the severity of the lick granuloma.

Ideally, the cause, if it can be determined, should be treated. Sometimes, it can be as simple as giving the dog more to do; a dog can cause a lick granuloma out of boredom. If the granuloma is severe, the dog may need a course of antibiotics. Meanwhile, the dog needs to be prevented from continuously licking the spot, which may mean fitting him for an Elizabethan collar (e-collar or "cone"). Alternatively, it's possible that simply putting a sock over the paw will work. I can't imagine my dog leaving a sock on her paw for very long, but some dogs might be fine. Some owners have had success using a foul-tasting chew deterrent, such as Bitter Apple, on the area, while others report success with acupuncture to ease the itching and help the granuloma heal.

37 Illnesses

Addison's Disease

Addison's disease, also known as hypoadrenocorticism, refers to a lack of cortin from the adrenal glands. Cortin includes several hormones that help regulate weight, mineral balance, the structure of connective tissue, some white blood cell production, and skin health. Addison's disease may be caused by an immune problem, or it may be brought on by pituitary cancer, which interrupts production of the hormones that trigger the adrenal glands. Addison's can also occur if a dog is taking a cortisone drug and then suddenly stops.

Symptoms of Addison's can be vague and may include vomiting, lethargy, and poor appetite. The only way to be positive that a dog has Addison's disease is with an adrenocorticotropic hormone (ACTH) response test. ACTH comes from the pituitary

gland. If the test does not stimulate the production of cortin, the dog has Addison's. As treatment, your veterinarian may give your dog fludrocortisone acetate or prescribe a corticosteroid like prednisone.

Bloat

Bloat is technically known as gastric dilation/ volvulus and is more common in large dogs, but any dog can be affected. With bloat, the stomach fills with gas and stretches, causing abdominal pain. Then, the stomach flips over on itself, cutting off both ends and making it impossible for any gas to escape. This also cuts off the blood supply to the stomach, and the dog will die if surgery is not performed as soon as possible. If bloat occurs in a large dog who has a high risk of it happening again, the veterinarian will tack the stomach to the abdominal wall to prevent further episodes.

It may help prevent bloat if you feed two or more meals a day instead of just one large meal. Some sources suggest that you wait an hour after meals before exercising your dog and that you wait an hour after strenuous exercise before feeding, but these factors don't really seem to make much difference.

"Speed eaters" seem to be more susceptible to bloat, so try to slow down the pace at which your dog gulps his food. Add water to the food, spread the kibble out on a plate, or add large rocks to your dog's dish so that he has to eat around them. Just be

Basset Hound puppy

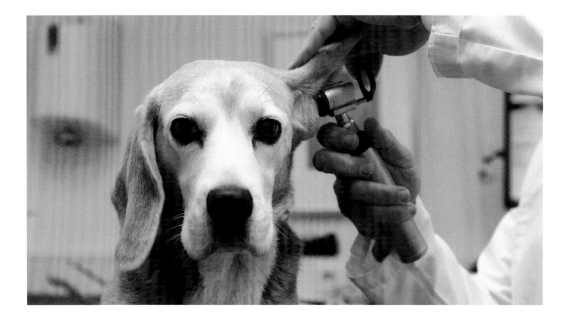

sure to use large enough rocks so that your dog doesn't eat them along with the food. Feeding your dog from raised dishes, although previously thought of as a bloat preventative, may actually increase the possibility of bloat.

Cushing's Disease

Cushing's disease, also called hyperadrenocorticism, is the opposite of Addison's. With Cushing's, which is caused by a tumor on the adrenal glands or pituitary gland, the adrenal glands produce too much cortin. Symptoms may include increased appetite, frequent drinking and urination, high blood pressure, hair loss, and muscle weakness. The dog may have a bulging, sagging abdomen. A blood test can diagnose

the problem, and the disease can be treated, but not cured. Drugs can ease the symptoms and improve quality of life. If the cause is a tumor on the adrenal glands, it may be possible to remove the tumor.

Epilepsy

Epilepsy can be inherited (idiopathic, or of an unknown cause), or a dog may develop seizures because of eating poison, a head injury, brain cancer, a stroke, kidney or liver disease, or high or low blood sugar. Some medicines may also cause seizures. Breeds more prone to idiopathic epilepsy include Australian Shepherds, Beagles, Belgian Tervurens, Border Collies, Collies, German Shepherd Dogs, and Labrador Retrievers.

Seizures are scary to watch, but never try to handle or restrain your dog during a seizure because many dogs will try to bite. Just move furniture or anything else that's in his way and make sure that he can't hurt himself.

If a seizure lasts too long, your dog may overheat. If you think your dog may be overheating, pour cool water on his feet and turn on a fan. Call your veterinarian after a seizure and schedule an appointment so that your vet can try to determine the cause of the seizure. Depending on the cause, seizures can be controlled with medication.

Hypothyroidism

Hypothyroidism is the inadequate production of thyroid hormone. If your dog has skin problems, is always hungry, has a coarse coat, is gaining weight, and is lethargic, it may be thyroid trouble. A simple blood test can

determine a thyroid problem, and a daily medicine can correct the problem.

Mange

Mange is caused by tiny mites and comes in two forms. Sarcoptic mange causes itching and, in advanced cases, skin lesions and hair loss. Ivermectin is used to treat it, and your veterinarian may also recommend sulfur dips. Treatment usually takes three weeks. The dog's bedding should be thoroughly disinfected or thrown away.

Demodectic mange is passed from mother to puppies and affects puppies between the ages of three and ten months. There may be a loss of hair around the eyes, lips, tips of ears, or forelegs. Ivermectin and special shampoos are used to treat it. In mild case, the mange may go away on its own. In severe cases, it may need up to a year of treatment.

Von Willebrand's Disease

Von Willebrand's is an inherited bleeding disorder in which the dog doesn't have adequate stores of the von Willebrand factor (vWF), which is a clotting factor. There is no cure, but thyroid supplements may increase the vWF in hypothyroid dogs. Fortunately, there is a test for von Willebrand's disease, and responsible breeders should test their breeding stock and not breed affected dogs.

Belgian Tervuren puppy

Fleas

Fleas are nasty little bugs that can torment your dog with their bites. They can make your dog's life miserable—and they're not averse to chomping on a human, either.

A single flea can bite your dog up to 400 times in just one day, and that same flea can produce over 200 eggs in a couple of days. If only a tenth of those eggs grow to be adults, your dog could be bitten 8,000 times a day! Besides the fact that they are sucking blood, fleas can also spread disease. Plus, if your dog is biting and scratching, he can cause surface wounds that can become infected. Many dogs are allergic to flea saliva, and they may need to be treated with antihistamines and/or antibiotics.

Dogs who swallow fleas in the process of chewing and licking at flea bites may acquire tapeworms. Tapeworms are the least harmful of the worms that may infest your dog, and they are easily treated, but it's better to prevent them from the start.

GIVE ME A BREAK!

If you live in northern areas with cold winters, you'll have a short break from fleas each year. If you live in a hot, dry area, you may not have a flea problem at all because the climate is too dry for fleas. If you live in a warmer, wetter climate, you may be facing a year-round battle.

If your dog is scratching and you suspect fleas, turn him over and inspect his stomach, especially toward the back legs, where the fur is thinner. Push the hair against the grain. You may see a flea or two scurrying for cover. Or, you may not see a flea at all, but you may notice flecks of flea dirt. If you're not sure if what you're looking at is flea dirt or just regular dirt, collect a bit on a piece of white paper or paper towel and wet it. If it turns reddish, it's flea dirt.

If you don't see anything on your dog but still suspect fleas, run a flea comb through his coat. Flea combs have very fine, closely set teeth that can trap fleas. Once you've determined that there are fleas, the war has begun. Be aggressive with flea control.

Daily vacuuming is as effective as any spray in keeping the flea population down in the house. Cut up a flea collar and put it in the vacuum bag to help kill the fleas. Also, change the vacuum bag frequently, or you'll be supporting a flea colony in the bag. Wash your dog's bed frequently because that is where most of the flea eggs will accumulate. Combing your dog with a flea comb will also help trap the unwanted guests.

A good bath will eliminate fleas but will not prevent them from reinfesting your dog. There is also a pill, Capstar, which acts within 30 minutes to kill the adult fleas on a dog. It's not a long-term preventative, but it can help to quickly kill fleas already on the dog.

CAT CAUTION

The ingredients in some parasite preventatives for dogs, such as K9 Advantix, are harmful to cats. If you have a cat and a dog, choose another type of preventative so that your cat doesn't accidentally come in contact with it while grooming her canine buddy or elsewhere in the home environment.

For long-term protection, talk to your veterinarian about what might be best for your dog. Program, an oral solution that you administer to your dog monthly, is a growth regulator rather than an insecticide. The flea absorbs it from your dog's blood, and the product prevents cocoons from forming, so flea larvae never develop into adults. Frontline is a monthly topical preventative that fights ticks as well as fleas. Advantage and K9 Advantix are other widely available monthly topical treatments. In addition to fighting fleas, Advantix also repels mosquitoes and ticks. NexGard is a monthly

chewable that protects against both ticks and fleas. Each of these preventatives has different active ingredients, so discuss with your vet which one is the safest and most effective for your dog.

Ticks

Ticks may or may not be a problem where you live, but, unfortunately, more and more areas that used to be almost tick-free are now seeing an invasion of the annoying little pests.

Remove a tick gently by pulling it straight out with tweezers and then disposing of it in alcohol to kill it. Never use a cigarette or anything else that will burn because you will likely burn your dog in the process. If you don't think you can remove the tick properly, or you don't want to try, have your veterinarian do it for you. It's important to check your dog on a routine basis if ticks are present in your area; you cannot leave them on your dog. Ticks can be hard to find, so be patient and thorough.

Reduce tick habitat in your yard by cutting back overgrown shrubs. Ticks like dark, moist places, so also get rid of any dead wood or piles of lawn debris. Consider using a chewable or topical tick preventative from your veterinarian. There is also a vaccine against Lyme disease that you should discuss with your vet. While antibiotics may cure a disease, preventing Lyme disease is the better course of action.

The Major Diseases Transmitted by Ticks in the United States

DISEASE	TYPE OF TICK	SYMPTOMS
Lyme disease	Black-legged tick (formerly called the deer tick)	Lameness, swollen joints, fever, fatigue, lack of appetite
Canine ehrlichiosis	Brown dog tick	Fever, lack of appetite, depression, weight loss, runny eyes and nose, nosebleeds, swollen limbs
Canine anaplasmosis	Black-legged tick	Fever, lack of appetite, stiff joints, lethargy, vomiting, diarrhea, possibly seizures
Rocky Mountain spotted fever	American dog tick, wood tick, and Lone Star tick	Fever, stiffness, neurological problems, skin lesions
Canine babesiosis	American dog tick, brown dog tick	Anemia, weakness, vomiting
Canine bartonellosis	Brown dog tick	Lameness, fever, possible heart or liver disease
Canine hepatozoonosis	Brown dog tick, Gulf Coast tick (spread by the dog ingesting the tick)	Fever, runny eyes and nose, muscle pain, bloody diarrhea

Mosquitoes

Mosquitoes spread heartworm, and this deadly parasite has been found in all fifty states, so no dog is safe from exposure. The treatment for heartworm can also be life-threatening, so prevention is the best option.

Heartworm larvae develop in mosquitoes and are passed to the dog when a mosquito bites him. These larvae then move into the chambers of the right side of the dog's heart, where they mature and produce microfilariae, which circulate in the dog's blood. Adult heartworms can completely fill the heart chambers of an infected dog, and an infected dog may tire easily and develop a cough.

Talk to your veterinarian about a monthly heartworm preventative for your dog. Some prevent only heartworms, but some also include ingredients that kill other parasitic worms, such as hookworms. There is also a shot available that is effective for up to six months. Your vet will perform an annual blood test before prescribing a preventative because he or she will want to first know that the dog is not infected with heartworm.

Keeping your dog on a preventative year-round is the best idea, but it will also help if you eliminate areas where mosquitoes breed, such as standing water. Keep your dog indoors at dawn and dusk, when mosquitoes are typically active.

39 Internal Parasites

Internal parasites, or worms, are usually detected via a fecal test done by your veterinarian. Fortunately, your veterinarian can prescribe medicines to get rid of worms in your dog. Also, you can choose a heartworm preventative that is effective against hook-, whip-, and roundworms as well.

Tapeworms are the least harmful and the most common of the internal parasites that affect dogs. Tapeworm segments are visible in the stool and will look like small grains of rice. Check your dog's stool periodically for evidence of tapeworms. Fleas can spread tapeworms, so take measures to keep the flea population down.

Hookworm eggs are passed in the feces of infected dogs and can live in the soil for a long time—and once they're in your yard, they are just about impossible to eradicate. Hookworms may also be passed from a mother to her puppies. Hookworms feed on blood and can cause fatal anemia in puppies if untreated.

Roundworms can also contaminate the soil for years. Most puppies are born with these worms because the larvae are able to live in an intermediate host—in this case, the mother—and not infect her. It's usually necessary to worm young puppies.

Dogs usually contract whipworms through infected soil and, once again, they are just about impossible to get rid of, short of paving your entire yard. If your dog has periodic bouts of diarrhea with mucus and blood

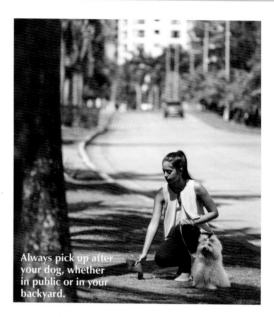

Always pick up after your dog, whether in public or in your backyard.

present, he may have whipworms, which cause deep inflammation of the colon.

We previously mentioned heartworms, which can cause a life-threatening infestation, and the treatment is almost as risky. If your dog does get heartworms, the first step is to get rid of the adult worms. This treatment involves arsenamide injected intravenously, twice a day, for two or three days. The worms die slowly and are carried to the lungs by the bloodstream, where they gradually disintegrate. This type of slow poison is preferred because if the worms were all killed immediately, a simultaneous embolism might prove fatal; even killing the worms slowly stresses the lungs and may cause permanent damage. Enforced rest for four to six weeks following treatment is the usual recovery time.

Dental care is not something usually associated with dogs, but statistics show that 75 percent of all dogs have some kind of periodontal problem by the time they are four years old. Although dogs are not as susceptible to tooth decay as humans are, they do develop plaque, which, if not removed, hardens to tartar. Tartar, in turn, can cause abscesses, and the bacteria from those abscesses can circulate in the system, leading to pneumonia or heart, liver, or kidney problems, which can lead to death. The bottom line is this: it's a good idea to take care of your dog's teeth, starting from the day you get him. It's not just a question of white teeth and fresh breath; it really can be a matter of life or death.

Dry food may help a little in preventing plaque, but many dogs barely chew their food at all. Hard biscuits can also help a bit, as can nylon bones and rawhide strips. Nylon bones get rough ends as they are chewed and act like toothbrushes. Rawhide can be good, but it requires supervision; many dogs shouldn't have rawhide at all because they bite off and swallow large chunks that can lead to intestinal blockages or stomach upset.

Real bones, if fresh and uncooked, can help keep your dog's teeth clean, but dogs who are aggressive chewers can end up with a mass of indigestible bone in the stomach, which can lead to vomiting or intestinal blockage.

One of the best things you can do is brush your dog's teeth—daily is ideal, but even once a week will help. This will be easier with a puppy, but even adult dogs can eventually get used to brushing.

Even with regular brushing, there may come a time when your dog needs a professional cleaning. Not all dogs are alike, of course. Some dogs may need their teeth cleaned every six months; some may go their entire lives without needing a professional cleaning. Have your veterinarian check your dog's teeth at least once a year. If you notice in between checkups that your dog's breath smells worse than his normal "dog breath," that he is drooling or pawing at his mouth, or that he is having trouble eating and no longer wants to chew on toys or bones, make an appointment with your veterinarian right away.

Start by wrapping a piece of gauze around your finger and rubbing gently over your dog's teeth and gums. This may work better if you flavor the gauze with a bit of hot dog or cheese. Praise your dog and give him a treat after each session. Go slow. You may be able to do only one small section initially, especially with an adult. When your dog is comfortable with having your gauze-wrapped finger in his mouth, graduate to a canine toothbrush. Some are similar to human toothbrushes, while others are made of rubber and slip onto the end of your index finger.

Beef- or chicken-flavored canine toothpaste may make your dog more willing to let you brush. On that note, always use a toothpaste especially for dogs. Because dogs don't rinse and spit the way people do, human toothpaste can make your dog sick.

A first-aid kit is something everyone should have, and many items you need in a canine first-aid kit are similar to those found in a kit for humans. You can buy a first-aid kit for dogs, or you can just stock some basics. If you don't have a special kit, designate one shelf in a cupboard for these supplies so that you know right where they are in an emergency. If you travel a lot, carry a small kit in your car with some essentials, such as antiseptic, gauze, and a few aspirin.

Some people include a muzzle in their dog's kit. Even the gentlest family pet may bite when in pain, and if you're worried about being bitten, you can't concentrate on helping your dog. You can even use a wide strip of gauze as a muzzle by wrapping the gauze around the dog's muzzle and tying the ends behind his ears. Never muzzle an unconscious dog or one who is having trouble breathing.

Another thing to remember is that a first-aid kit is not a substitute for veterinary care. They are fine for minor injuries or to help stabilize the dog for a trip to the vet, but a first-aid kit is not a do-it-yourself fix for broken bones, heavy bleeding, or deep cuts or puncture wounds.

Following are useful items for your dog's first-aid kit:

- Activated charcoal. Give this orally if your dog has eaten something that you suspect is poisonous; the charcoal helps neutralize the poison. *Note*: This is not the same as the charcoal you use to barbecue. Ask your pharmacist for the right kind of charcoal.
- Adhesive tape and/or veterinary wrap. Adhesive tape will work to hold a bandage

or splint in place in a pinch, but it will also pull your dog's fur. Veterinary wrap, available from pet-supply stores or online retailers, won't stick to fur.

- Antibiotic ointment. I use a triple antibiotic cream, available at any drug store, on scrapes and shallow cuts. It's also good for hot spots.
- Artificial tears. If you've been somewhere dry and windy, artificial tears can soothe irritated eyes.
- Benadryl. Use this for allergic reactions, such as a bug bite or bee sting. Give one milligram per pound of body weight.
- Children's aspirin. Give one children's aspirin per 10 to 15 pounds of body weight for fever or pain. Don't give your dog ibuprofen or acetaminophen.

- Cotton balls or a roll of cotton, for applying salves or liquid external medicines.
- Gauze. A roll of gauze can secure dressings. Various sizes of gauze pads are also handy for covering wounds.
- Hemostats and/or tweezers. Either of these items can be used to remove splinters as well as larger pieces of debris that may be in a wound.
- Hydrocortisone ointment. This is useful if your dog has bug bites or a rash.
- Hydrogen peroxide. You can use this to clean and disinfect a wound, and you can also use it to induce vomiting; give 5 milliliters (1 teaspoon) orally per 10 pounds of body weight. If you have a large bottle, you won't need Ipecac syrup.

CAUTION
Never induce vomiting if your dog has swallowed something caustic.

- Ipecac syrup. Give by mouth to induce vomiting.
- Kaopectate helps control diarrhea. Give 1 teaspoon per 5 pounds of body weight. Repeat dosage every four hours.
- Oral syringes. It's much easier to administer medicines with an oral syringe than with a spoon. Stock 3-, 6-, and 12-centimeter syringes.
- Rubber gloves. They're not a necessity, but they can make dealing with something messy a bit more pleasant.
- Scissors. Use for cutting gauze and vet wrap and for trimming fur away from a wound.
- Thermometer. Your dog's normal temperature will be between 100 and 102.5 degrees Fahrenheit. This should go without saying, but you'll need to take your dog's temperature rectally, not orally.
- Veterinarian's phone number. Keep that number, and the number of the closest emergency clinic, with your first-aid supplies as well as programmed into your cell phone.

- Veterinary first-aid manual. Keep one on hand; it can be helpful in an emergency.

If you'd prefer some holistic choices for first aid care, here are a few that can be useful.

- Aloe vera can help to relieve pain and itching from hot spots, insect bites or stings, and other skin irritations. It has a bitter taste, so it might help discourage your dog from licking and biting at an injured area.
- Arnica gel for use on sprains and bruises.
- Calendula gel promotes healing of scrapes and shallow wounds.
- Cayenne pepper can be used to stop bleeding.
- Comfrey ointment is another helpful product for minor scrapes and injuries.
- Rescue Remedy is a mixture of five of the single Bach flower essences and is used to treat shock, collapse, or trauma.

Coming Home and Settling In

Whether you are getting a puppy or an adult dog, bringing him home will be an adjustment for both of you. With a puppy, he will be away from his littermates and mother for the first time. Your house will be a strange place, with strange smells, strange people, and maybe other animals—all a bit overwhelming. Be patient. Things may not go smoothly that first day, but it will all work out eventually. While an adult may settle in more quickly, the following advice pertains to both adults and puppies.

First, plan to pick up your puppy when you'll have some time to help him settle in. Get him on a Friday night, for instance, so that you'll have two days to help him get adjusted before everyone goes back to school or work. Getting a puppy during summer break or school vacations can be a good idea because, if you have children, they'll be available to help care for the puppy and keep him on a regular schedule for housetraining.

The belief used to be that Christmas was the absolute worst time to get a puppy, and many breeders still refuse to sell puppies right before Christmas. However, the San Francisco SPCA has found that the number of dogs returned after being adopted at Christmastime is no greater than at other times of the year. However, if your house is "Holiday Central," and you're hosting all of the relatives or a big neighborhood party, it's probably best to wait on getting the dog. Likewise, if you have very young children,

it might be better to wait. Children can get pretty wound up over the holidays, and your new puppy needs things to be relatively calm so he can adjust to all the newness with a minimum of stress.

Whenever you get your puppy, be prepared beforehand. Have a supply of whatever food he's used to, food and water bowls, and a collar and leash for those trips outdoors. Have an appropriately sized crate, too. The enclosed space will make him feel more secure and, when you're not watching him, the crate will keep him safe.

Try to keep things relatively calm. Don't invite all of the relatives and neighbors to see the puppy when he first comes home. Let him get used to you and the family. Certainly, the children should pet and hold him, but leave the roughhousing for later.

Give him time for naps. Puppies, like babies, need their rest. Review the housetraining tips in this book and start following them. The fewer accidents your puppy has indoors, the faster he'll learn that outdoors is the place to go.

Be prepared: the first night or two may be the hardest. When everyone settles down and the house gets quiet, your puppy may really feel the loneliness. A stuffed toy that the puppy can snuggle with may help. You might consider a Snuggle Puppy (www.smartpetlove.com), which is a stuffed toy with a heating unit and a "heartbeat," designed to help the puppy feels comfortable, as if he's back with his litter.

Some puppies cry; some may settle right in. One of my dogs, Griffin, cried for fifteen or twenty minutes each night for his first two weeks. With his crate right next to the bed, he was hard to ignore, and the sound was heart-wrenching. Yes, I could have taken him into bed with me, but that would have started a habit that I didn't want to encourage. I love sharing my bed with a dog now and then, but I didn't want to make our bed Griffin's official sleeping spot. I also didn't want to risk a potty accident in the bed. It's easier to clean a crate than to change the sheets and wash a mattress pad.

Anyway, your dog will get used to being alone, and yes, you will live through it. Your puppy may sleep through the night, but don't count on it. If he does sleep straight through, his definition of "morning" may be earlier than yours. Gael woke me faithfully at 5:30 a.m. for her first two months with us.

Middle-of-the-night wake-up calls are a good reason to keep your puppy's crate in your bedroom. You can get up and get the puppy out as soon as you hear the whimpers, thus avoiding an accident and helping the housetraining process along. Don't dawdle. When you hear that cry in the night, get up, grab your robe, pick up the puppy, and head for the great outdoors. As your puppy grows, so will his bladder, so these midnight potty trips won't last forever, even if it feels like it.

If you're fortunate to spend the first week at home with the puppy, you'll get a good start on housetraining and leash training. You'll want a small, flat, buckle collar for your puppy and, although some puppies may act as though the collar is torture, most will adjust with just a few scratches at it. Fasten a lightweight leash to the collar and let the puppy drag it around and get used to it. Supervise this—you don't want the leash getting caught on something, and you don't want the puppy to start chewing on it.

Eventually, you can pick up the end and start following the puppy around. Don't try to steer him; just follow along. Do the same when you take him into the yard. Encourage him to follow you by calling him and slapping your leg. If you sound happy and excited, he's likely to come running. Don't drag the puppy. If he starts to pull backward, walk toward him to release any pressure and start again. If you must, just pick him up to take him back inside.

Your puppy's first week will likely be one of the toughest, but it will all be worth it for the joy of adding a canine companion to the family who will be with you for the next ten or more years.

43 Introducing the Kids

Kids and dogs go together like peanut butter and jelly, but, unlike the sandwich, you can't just throw them together if you want the best results. Never, ever leave a young child and a dog unsupervised. Babies and toddlers make fast, jerky movements and may make high-pitched noises, both of which can trigger the prey drive in a dog. Young children don't always understand that they may be hurting a dog, so it's up to you to keep everyone safe. Don't let children stand or sit on the dog, no matter his size, and don't let them pull on his ears or tail or poke his eyes. Learn enough about canine body language to know when your dog is getting stressed so that you can remove him from the situation. Don't let children interfere with your dog when he is eating or sleeping. Crating your dog can help minimize risk.

Encourage your child to sit on the floor to play with the puppy rather than trying to pick the puppy up. Teach older children the proper way to pick up a puppy, with one hand under the chest and the other supporting the hindquarters. The older your puppy gets, the more he'll enjoy playing with children and the rowdier the play can be, but always be alert to any play that looks like it could become dangerous.

Another good way to help grow the bond between your children and the dog is to let them help take care of him. Even a small child can fill the dog's water dish or help walk the dog. However, while it's fine for a small child to have a hand on the leash, never entrust the dog to a small child. Even a small dog can pull a lead out of a child's hand or even knock the child over. Keep everyone safe and remember

that even though your children may enjoy caring for the dog, it's up to you to make sure that your dog isn't neglected because the children forgot or were too busy.

If you don't have children, it's a good idea to introduce your puppy to some while he's young. You'll want your dog to be comfortable around both adults and children. Maybe there are some neighborhood children who'd like to meet your puppy. Just remember to supervise all interaction. You want this to be a positive experience for both the puppy and the children.

Another good way to socialize your puppy is to visit a local shopping center. Ask people to gently pet your dog and give him a treat. A friendly person, leaning over to give him a pat and offer him a treat, will help your dog understand that people are the source of good things. Don't let your dog become overwhelmed.

If you've adopted an adult dog from a rescue, the rescue volunteers can probably tell you whether or not he is good with children. If you're adopting from a shelter, you may not know whether your new dog is good around children. Always err on the side of caution. Make introductions slowly and with the dog on a leash, but keep the leash slack. Make sure the child understands to move slowly and quietly and not to pat the dog on the head because a hand descending suddenly toward his head may frighten a dog, and he may snap or bite. If you're not sure of a dog, keep babies and toddlers away from him entirely.

Some small treats, quietly offered, may be the start of a beautiful friendship—but a small word of warning on having anyone give your dog a treat: some dogs take treats more gently than others. I had two male Corgis who were very good around children, but neither ever learned to take a treat gently. If your dog isn't gentle when taking treats, have the child drop the treat rather than hold it out for the dog to take.

This may seem like a strange topic in a book aimed at people who don't currently have dogs, but you may have dogs who visit, you may want your dog to meet other dogs in the neighborhood, or you may enjoy having a dog so much that you get another one. There's no way to know what any individual dog will do or how he will react upon meeting another dog. Supervised introductions will make things go more smoothly.

If you have a new puppy, plan to introduce him to an adult dog in a neutral area. Your yard is better than the house. Don't put a lead on the adult dog. The owner might unconsciously pull on the lead, and that can signal to the dog that he needs to be defensive. If there are multiple adults for the puppy to meet, do it one dog at a time. Make sure there are no toys or treats around that an older dog might want to guard. If you're introducing an adult to an adult, put leads on the dogs, but make sure that the leads are completely slack or don't hold them at all. Then, you'll be able to grab your dog's lead if needed.

If, for any reason, you are afraid that an adult dog might harm your puppy, keep the puppy in your arms. Sit or stand quietly and let the older dog sniff the puppy. If the older dog looks like he's going to try to grab or bite your puppy, you'll be able to turn away. If you're afraid for both you and the puppy, skip the introduction altogether.

My adult Corgis were always fine around puppies. My males thought they were wonderful, my oldest female considered them hers to boss around and discipline, and another of my females acted as if she had no idea what they were. I did bring home one adult male rescue, and he and my female were fine together. She basically ignored him, both indoors and out.

If you already have a cat in residence, introductions between cat and puppy will take some time. Yes, it's possible that your cat will welcome the puppy with delight, but it's not likely. Don't just let nature take its course or you're likely to end up with a terrified, cowering puppy.

One tip that might help get the cat used to the idea of a dog is to have a friend with a cat-friendly dog come to visit before your dog comes home. Keep the dog leashed and just let the cat get used to the idea of a dog in the house. The dog and cat may never even meet; the cat may just hide, but at least he will have experienced a dog in the house, which may help with introductions to your new dog later on.

When it is time to introduce your new dog to your cat, set things up so that both cat and puppy are safe and can get used to each other gradually. For initial introductions, put the cat in a separate room and close the door. Let the dog and cat smell each other through the crack under the door. When you let the puppy loose, put the cat in a separate room. When the cat is out, have your puppy in his crate or in an exercise pen. Let the cat approach at his own pace, getting used to the puppy's smell. Maybe they'll touch noses through the wire, maybe not. Offer treats to both when they tolerate the other. Give your cat treats if he approaches calmly and doesn't hiss or scratch. Depending on the size and age of your dog, keep him on a lead when he is not in his crate or in a pen so that he can't overwhelm the cat with his exuberance.

OTHER FURRY FRIENDS

If you have other pets, such as rabbits, gerbils, or hamsters, it's likely that they will never be buddies with your dog. Your dog will see these smaller animals as prey. Make sure that smaller pets are in safe cages out of your dog's reach. Yes, there are cute videos on YouTube of dogs cuddling with rabbits or with a hamster perched on a dog's head, but these are not the norm. Even if your dog seems just fine sniffing at your guinea pig through its cage bars, he might not act the same way when the guinea pig is loose and running around. Keep all of your pets safe.

Make sure your cat can always get away from the dog. Use baby gates in doorways; cats can generally leap these easily, leaving the puppy behind. Clear a shelf or two and remove items from your fireplace mantel so that the cat has someplace high and safe where he can rest undisturbed. Keep the litter box in a room that is a "puppy-free" zone. Again, a baby gate across the doorway may work. It's not fair to your cat to have to try to use the litter box while a puppy is bouncing and poking, and it's a good idea to keep the litter box where the puppy can't get at it anyway. Many dogs seem to find litter-box deposits tasty.

Be patient. Total acceptance is not likely to happen in just a day or two. It can take weeks. Make sure neither animal can harass the other when you're not around. Supervise their meetings and praise both animals when they are calm and nonthreatening. Many dogs and cats become best buddies, but even a truce can work as long as there are safety zones for everyone.

There are many ways to identify your dog as yours. If you are getting a purebred, you should get registration papers from the breeder, listing you as the owner. Your dog's breed, sex, and color will be listed as well. This is a legal document that proves your ownership of the dog. If you are adopting a mixed breed, you may get some kind of paperwork from the shelter or rescue organization.

However, these documents, although useful in proving ownership, won't help you get your dog back if he becomes lost. For that, there needs to be something connected to the dog that supplies the necessary information for getting him back to you. Using one or more forms of identification may increase the speed with which your dog is returned home.

One form of identification is a tattoo. Racing Greyhounds are routinely tattooed in the ear. Before microchipping became common, breeders would tattoo their dogs, frequently with the dog's registration number. Of course, that assumes that the finder of the dog knows how to use that number to find the owner. Some breeders would use their own Social Security numbers, but today, with identity theft prevalent, that's not a great idea. The other drawback to a tattoo, usually placed on the inner thigh of the dog, is that, as the dog grows, the area stretches and the number gets harder to read. Also, hair may grow over it, hiding it from view. And would the finder know to look at the dog's inner thigh?

Most dogs wear collars with tags that can help return a lost dog to his owners. All dogs, by law, must be vaccinated for rabies, and you'll receive a rabies tag to fasten to your dog's collar. The number on that tag can be used to trace the dog back to you.

When you register your dog with the town or city in which you live, which is required by most municipalities, you'll receive a license tag with a number that will lead back to you. Many people add a tag with their own information, making it easy for whoever finds the dog to contact them. This ID tag may include the dog's name and the owner's address and cell phone number, although just a phone number is sufficient and probably safer.

All of these tags are helpful, but what happens if your dog's collar comes off? It could get caught on something, or someone could remove it. The advantage of microchipping is that the dog can't lose the chip. A microchip is a small chip, about the

CHIP TIP

Occasionally, a chip may "travel" in the body and not maintain its position between the shoulder blades. During an office visit, ask your vet to scan your dog to make sure the chip hasn't moved or, if it has, to find out where it is.

company, in turn, contacts you. There's also a registry called PetKey (www.petkey.com) that registers chips from all companies, no matter what company has issued it.

A microchip is one of the best forms of identification you can have. Yes, attach your dog's tags to his collar, but get that chip, too. Chips can't get lost or damaged, and as long as you keep your contact information up to date, the microchip offers the best chance that you'll get your dog back if he's ever lost.

size of a grain of rice, that is injected under your dog's skin, between the shoulder blades. Each chip has a number and is registered with whatever microchip company you choose. A scanner, which most veterinary offices and shelters have, reads the chip. Once read, the issuing company is contacted, and the

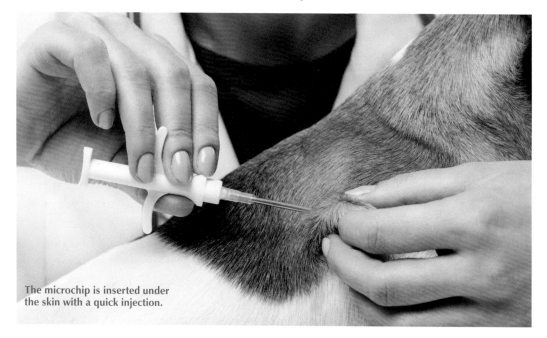

The microchip is inserted under the skin with a quick injection.

Deciding beforehand where your puppy will eliminate, eat, and sleep will make his first few weeks easier. An adult dog will also benefit from consistency and routine as he adjusts to a new home.

You will want your new pal to learn quickly where it is appropriate to eliminate, whether you want to train your dog to go outdoors or, with a small dog, you'll be using a litter box or puppy pads. In addition to sticking to a potty schedule with your dog, always take him to the same area. Dogs are guided by scent, and if they've gone somewhere once, they're more likely to go there again. That's why, if your puppy has an accident in the house, you want to thoroughly clean that spot to eliminate the odor so that the puppy won't be tempted to use that spot again.

When it comes to puppy's mealtimes, most people find it convenient to feed their dog in the kitchen, where there's an easy-to-clean floor in case of spills. If you have multiple pets, feeding in the crate or in a separate room may make more sense. Wherever you choose, make sure it's away from household traffic and that your dog is left alone to eat. While no one wants a dog who growls and guards his food, a dog should be allowed to eat without being pestered by people or other pets. My own dogs eat in about forty-five seconds, so giving them a little space and quiet doesn't disrupt our lives very much.

You may have read that you should always eat your own meal first before feeding the dog to let the dog know that you're the leader. This theory has been debunked, and, in my experience, it really doesn't matter whether you feed your dog before or after you eat. Do what fits your schedule best. In the morning, I feed my dogs first, freeing me to read the paper at my leisure and relax over my breakfast without thinking about when I need to feed them. In the evening, I tend to feed them after I've eaten. On the occasions when I've fed them before our dinner, they are content to nap while we're eating our meal. After more than thirty-five years of dog ownership, no dogs have taken over the house, and they still obey me when I ask them to sit, come, or stay.

My own personal rule is no begging at the table, so none of my dogs has ever been fed tidbits from the table. If you want to eat all your meals with a dog staring at you pathetically or nudging your arm, go ahead and give your dog treats from your plate. If not, don't start. It's up to you. Dogs are opportunists, and if you give them an inch, they will gladly take the remaining mile.

As your dog adjusts to family life, he may choose different sleeping spots, but, as a puppy, or even with an adult, until you are sure you can trust him with the run of the house, you need to choose where your dog sleeps. A puppy, especially, should be crated overnight. He will feel secure, and he will be safe. If you can put the puppy's crate in your room, so much the better. You'll hear him if he needs to go out during the night, and it's another opportunity for him to bond to the family. He gets to be with you for eight uninterrupted (maybe!) hours.

You may decide that you want your new pal to sleep with you, and that's OK, too, once he's housetrained. Before you get in the habit of letting your puppy sleep in your bed, think about how big he will be as an adult. You may not want to share your bed with a fully grown St. Bernard, especially when it's hot and humid. Also, it's been my experience that dogs rarely sleep in line with a human but rather sleep across the bed, taking up most of the space.

If you do decide to allow the dog on the bed, make it by invitation only. This is your space, and you don't want your dog claiming it as his own, trying to convince you to sleep elsewhere.

Many people have dogs their entire lives and never have a fenced yard. People in apartment buildings may not even have a yard. People without fenced yards take their dogs for walks daily and in all types of weather. I enjoy walking my dogs, but I also enjoy having a fenced yard. It's especially handy for the early-morning and late-night trips outdoors. I like being able to just open the door and let the dogs out. Later in the day, the fenced yard provides a safe area where we can play fetch.

Fencing comes in all kinds of materials and at all kinds of prices. The good thing about fencing is that it is usually a one-time expense. The cheapest fencing is wire fencing, which comes in many different mesh sizes. Some types hook onto metal posts pounded into the ground. At one of our previous homes, the fencing had openings about 4 inches square and was supported on a wooden framework. This worked well for our dogs but would not have been good for very small dogs who could squeeze through the openings, nor would it have been sufficient for most terriers, who could easily dig underneath the fence. Some wrought iron, aluminum, or wooden picket fencing may be fine for larger dogs who can't squeeze between the bars, but the fence might have to be much taller to keep the dog from jumping out.

We have always opted for a 6-foot-tall fence, even though my dogs are barely 12

inches tall at the shoulder. While my current dogs would probably be fine with a shorter fence, I've had Corgis who could easily jump a 3-foot fence and, with enough temptation, would. Also, a short fence means that, while it might keep my dogs in, it might not keep other dogs out. A 3-foot fence means that if someone wanted to steal a dog, he or she could easily get over the fence, grab the dog, and get back out. I recommend 4 feet as the minimum fence height for a yard with dogs.

Chain link is a popular choice that has worked well for us. If you have terriers, though, you may need to bury fencing a few feet underground. Remember, terriers were bred to dig, and it doesn't take long for a terrier to dig under a fence.

Vinyl or PVC fencing is attractive and never needs painting. It's also probably one of the most expensive fencing choices. At another of our previous homes, we used vinyl fencing facing the sidewalk and used chain link along the sides and back, where there were fewer distractions for the dogs to bark at. At our current home, we have neighbors and thus a solid wood fence on the theory that the less the dogs can see, the less they'll bark.

If you have a yard with wire fencing, and your dog is constantly charging the fence after anything that passes, consider planting

Fences keep dogs in and unwanted visitors out.

bushes at the appropriate places. This will not only help block sight lines and keep the dog farther back, it will also help muffle barking.

Many people use electronic fences and have very good luck with them. I don't use them because, while they may keep your dog in, they do not keep anything else out. We have a neighbor with two large Labrador Retrievers who often run loose. I wouldn't want them in my yard, possibly injuring one of my dogs.

I know that there are skunks living nearby, and, so far, the fence has kept them out of our yard. We also have deer in the area, and I don't want to have to deal with a deer–dog confrontation, which leads me to the other reason I won't use an electronic fence: if a dog has enough motivation—chasing a deer, for example—he will cross the fence line, ignoring the shock in favor of the chase. Once the chase is over, if the dog comes home, he will be reluctant to cross the line back into the yard and receive another shock. So, now your dog is outside the fence and won't come home.

Whatever kind of fencing you choose, never leave your dog outdoors when you're not at home. It's all too easy for someone to steal your dog from the yard, and it's all too easy for dogs to get into some kind of trouble when left alone. Even if that trouble is just barking, you'll have unhappy neighbors if you're gone for several hours.

Now that you have the yard fenced, you'll need cleanup tools. The same way that cat owners have scoops to clean litter boxes, you'll need tools to keep your yard picked up. Pet-supply stores sell "poop scoop" sets, with one tool that resembles a dustpan with a long handle, and the other a flat-bladed tool or small rake, again with a long handle. You use the flat blade or rake to push the feces into the dustpan and then dump it. I've designated a small garbage can lined with a trash bag for dog droppings. If you have a small dog, it may be just as easy for you to use a small plastic bag and then dump the contents (not the bag) into your toilet and flush.

Whether you have your own fenced-in yard or you walk your dog around the neighborhood, pick up after your dog. No one, not even other dog owners, wants to see—or, worse—step in, a mess your dog has made. You don't want to live with the smell or the flies that your dog's waste will attract to your yard, as well as, by extension, the germs those flies may bring into your house.

For walks, I use plastic sandwich bags, or you can reuse plastic grocery bags. If you have a very large dog, you might prefer a small portable scoop that you can carry on a walk. Some scoops close around the waste, and you can empty it when you return home, either into your toilet or a garbage can. You can even buy attachments for your leash that hold empty bags and full ones for hands-free carrying. However you want to pick up after your dog, be a responsible owner and do it.

Years ago, when many dogs, especially hunting dogs, were kept in packs and all lived in kennels or a barns, housetraining wasn't much of a concern. Today, when almost all dogs are house pets, housetraining is an important step. Some breeds may take longer than others to housetrain, but if you are persistent, patient, and consistent, you should be able to housetrain the family's new addition.

I'm using the term "puppy" here, but any dog can be trained, and rescue dogs often need a refresher course. With an adult dog, you won't need to make quite as many trips outdoors, but it's still good to set a schedule and to take your dog out frequently.

A crate can help speed up the housetraining process. Dogs instinctively don't want to soil their beds, so if you crate your puppy when you can't watch him, he'll have fewer accidents in the house and that means fewer chances to get in the habit of going indoors. The other advantage of the crate is that if your puppy does have an accident, it will be in a small, easy-to-clean area, not in the middle of your expensive rug.

Using the crate doesn't mean to crate the puppy and forget him. If your puppy is crated for too long, he will have no choice but to go in his crate, and this will definitely set back your progress in housetraining. Never leave a puppy crated for more than four hours at

the most—with very young puppies, make that two hours. Puppies are small, and so are their bladders. They can't physically hold it for very long. They can learn control, though, and following a schedule helps them learn that control.

Make sure that everyone in the family understands the importance of a regular schedule when they are with the puppy. You might even want to post the schedule on your refrigerator door. It might look something like the chart below. Or, your own schedule may look very different.

PUPPY POTTY SCHEDULE

6:00 a.m.	Take puppy out. Carry the puppy to the designated spot in the yard.
6:15 a.m.	Feed the puppy.
6:30 a.m.	Take the puppy out.
6:40–7:00 a.m.	Play with the puppy.
7:00 a.m.	Take the puppy out and then put him in his crate and get ready for work or school.
8:00 a.m.	Take the puppy out one more time before leaving for work or school.
12:00 p.m.	Take the puppy out.
12:10 p.m.	Feed the puppy and then crate the puppy while eating your lunch.
12:30 p.m.	Take the puppy out. Play with the puppy if there's time, but only after he's gone to the bathroom.
3:00 p.m.	Kids home from school. Take the puppy out. Play with the puppy after he's gone to the bathroom. Take the puppy out again.
5:30 p.m.	Take the puppy out. Feed the puppy. Crate the puppy while making dinner and eating. Take the puppy out again.
7:00 p.m.	Take the puppy out. Play with the puppy after he's gone to the bathroom.
11:00 p.m.	Take the puppy out one last time.

that's your cue to get up and out with him. Keep your coat and boots handy if it's winter. Remember to carry the puppy through the house and snap his lead on before going out. The middle of the night in a snowstorm is not when you want to be chasing a frisky puppy.

Another thing to remember is consistency with what door you use to go out and come in. Always take your puppy in and out the same door while training. Also take your dog to the same spot in the yard each time because the scent at this spot will remind him why he's there. In the beginning, you can mark the

For instance, if you don't have children, maybe you can rearrange your work schedule for a month or two so that your puppy gets the necessary breaks. Or, maybe there's a neighbor who can help you with the midday breaks if you're at work all day. The main thing is to have a schedule, be consistent, and take your puppy out often. The fewer accidents your puppy has indoors, the sooner he will understand that he needs to go outdoors every time.

Also, while your puppy may sleep through the night, don't count on it. If he wakes up at three in the morning and starts whining,

SLOW AND STEADY

Remember that slower is faster when it comes to housetraining. Don't give your puppy access to the entire house until you know he's trained. The more freedom he has, the more chance there is for an accident. Give it a week or two with no indoor accidents before opening up the entire house to your puppy, and, even then, keep a watchful eye on your pal. The excitement about and interest in the new environment may mean an accident or two. Be consistent and build a routine, and it shouldn't take more than a month to housetrain the new member of your family.

correct place yourself. If you wipe up an accident with an old rag, put that cloth out in the yard and then take your puppy to that spot when you go out.

While you're training, always go out with your puppy and always take him on a lead. That way, you can steer him to the correct area and keep him in that area until he's eliminated. If you just let him run out into the yard, he may become distracted with new sights and sounds and won't remember that he has to go until he gets back inside. It's fine to unsnap that lead and play with your puppy in the fenced yard, but do it after he's relieved himself.

Always praise your puppy when he goes where you want him to. Don't worry about what the neighbors might think. Go crazy over your puppy. Give him a treat or reward him with a play session.

WHAT NOT TO DO
First, *do not rub your dog's nose in urine or feces*! It doesn't teach the dog anything except to avoid you at all costs. Dogs have no idea why you're doing it. It's mean and pointless.

Second, *do not smack your puppy with a rolled-up newspaper (or anything else) if he has an accident in the house.* Instead, smack yourself for not noticing that your dog needed to go out. It's not always easy to tell with puppies, and many will just squat and "go," but, if you're alert, you'll see the puppy start to circle and sniff, searching for just the right spot. That's when you need to scoop him up or, if an adult dog, hurry him outside. Don't try to call your puppy to come to you. Just pick him up, or it will be too late.

You'll soon learn what clues, if any, your puppy uses to indicate that he needs to be taken out. Don't just wait until you see the signs, though. Take your puppy outside to his designated potty area when he wakes up in the morning or from a nap, after play sessions, and after meals.

If you're just not home often enough during the day to make using a crate practical for housetraining, paper-train your dog. If you have a very small dog and/or you live on an upper floor of an apartment building, you may want to have your dog use paper all the time. Litter boxes and indoor dog "stations" are other alternatives. Some people who live in high-rise apartment buildings like their dogs to have experience going on paper in case there's a power failure and the elevator is out of commission.

To paper-train your puppy so that he eventually learns to go outside, either use an exercise pen or confine your puppy to one specific room. A laundry room, kitchen, or bathroom is a good choice because these rooms usually have easy-to-clean linoleum flooring. Just be aware that your puppy may consider linoleum a wonderful chew toy. I don't understand how dogs can even get a grip on pieces of linoleum, but trust me, they can.

Cover the entire floor of the room with several layers of newspaper. Supply water and toys. If the area is big enough, you can even include the dog's crate, but remove the door. When you clean up, remove the top few layers of paper, leaving the lower layers, and then put fresh paper on top of those lower layers. Enough scent will remain to tell the puppy where to go.

After several days, cover a smaller area of the floor with paper. If your puppy

consistently uses the paper rather than the bare floor, reduce the area covered by newspapers even more. Continue this process until you've removed all of the paper. Don't rush the process, or you'll have to start back at the beginning.

During this time, continue to take the puppy outside when you are home. By the time you've reached the stage where there are no newspapers, your puppy should be making the connection that outdoors is where he needs to go. Keep him confined to his "paper room" during the day when you can't watch him and put down papers if he regresses.

If you have a small dog and you never intend to take him out to relieve himself on a regular basis, paper train as previously described, but never take up that final small area of paper. You can even use a low plastic box and line it with sheets of paper, keeping everything contained and making cleanup easier.

If you have a small dog, you also have the option of litter-box training. You'll need a litter box made for dogs, complete with doggy litter. Litter box training is the same as housetraining, following a set schedule and using a crate, but instead of taking the dog outdoors, take him to the litter box.

If you won't be using a crate but are enclosing the dog in a small room or ex-pen, spread newspapers on the floor and include the litter box in the room or enclosure. Spread a fine layer of litter on top of the newspaper. Gradually shrink the area covered with paper, closing in on the litter box, until you've removed all of the paper and only the litter box is left. When you're home, put the dog in the litter box whenever you think he might need it—after play, when waking from naps and first thing in the morning, and after meals.

As with cat litter boxes, your dog's litter box needs to be scooped regularly and thoroughly scrubbed at least once a week. With the litter box, the ban on products containing ammonia is lifted because if won't matter if the dog smells the ammonia; the box is where you want him to go anyway.

Another alternative is a special dog potty area. These feature artificial turf with a tray to collect liquid waste. The training process is the same; take the dog to the turf and praise when he uses it. Be patient, consistent, and persistent, and you'll soon have a dog reliably trained to go in whatever area you've chosen.

51 Puppy-Proofing

Before you bring home your puppy, make sure your house is ready for him. Puppies are like toddlers, only more so. They will put anything and everything into their mouths as they learn about the world around them. Once their teeth start to come in and they are teething, not only will they put anything in their mouths, they will chew on everything. Anything and everything is fair game to a teething puppy. Puppies are fast, and even if you think you're watching your puppy, he can get into trouble quickly. That's why crates are so handy for those times when you just can't devote all of your attention to watching the puppy.

Puppy-proofing is a lot like baby-proofing. Make sure nothing toxic or caustic is where a puppy might come in contact with it.

Electrical cords can be deadly if a puppy chews them. Run them behind furniture and, if there are some that are out in the open, consider running them through a length of PVC pipe.

Wastebaskets and trash cans may need to be put out of reach. The kitchen garbage may contain harmful foods or choking hazards, and the plastic garbage bag can suffocate a puppy. Bathroom wastebaskets can also contain things you don't want your dog to eat. My Corgi puppies were too small to be able to knock over the kitchen garbage, and they never seemed to care about the smaller wastebasket that stood next to my desk—until Griffin came along. He loved to knock over that basket and shred the paper in it. Finally, I just stopped using it, but he still thought it was great fun to knock it over, even if it was empty.

Furniture or rugs, especially those with fringe, may be particularly attractive to a puppy. If you have an expensive carpet, this might be the time to roll it up and put it away until your puppy is housetrained and has all of his adult teeth. Put breakables out of reach on sturdy shelves. A rambunctious puppy may sideswipe a table, sending fragile items tumbling. While you may not be able to move all of the books from a bookcase, if you've got valuable first editions, put them up on a higher shelf and leave the romance paperbacks for your puppy to gnaw on.

Your puppy may consider wooden chair and table legs the best possible teething toys, and you may not be able to prevent some damage. If an end table is very valuable, maybe it should go to the attic for a few months. Hayley was one of the best puppies we ever had in terms of not chewing things, but even she managed to leave her mark on the rung of an antique chair. Gael as a puppy thought that the oak legs of our dining table were delicious, and it's amazing how deep those puppy teeth can bite.

Train everyone in the family to always put away shoes and slippers. Pliable leather is always a favorite chew toy, as are socks, sweaters, and underwear. The only thing Hayley ever chewed, besides the one chair rung, was one of my husband's shoes—twice. After that, my husband remembered to always put away his shoes. And, speaking of shoes, don't ever give your puppy an old shoe or slipper as a toy. A puppy doesn't know the difference between an old worn-out shoe and brand new Nikes, fresh from the box.

Chewing is something dogs need to do. Don't punish your puppy for chewing; instead, provide alternatives to your possessions. Protect everything as best you can, provide plenty of dog toys, and watch the puppy as much as possible. When your dog is a staid old man, you'll look at those teeth marks on the dining room table and smile.

Dogs are worth all of the icky stuff, but it's always good to be prepared. Before you get a dog, you might as well buy stock in a paper towel company! You'll use paper towels for so many things, including picking up anything connected in any way to your dog. I've wasted many paper towels picking up what turned out to be sock fuzz, but I stand by my decision to never pick up anything with my bare hands.

This all started when I picked up a dead and thoroughly chewed mouse that one of my dogs had brought into the house. I don't know what I thought it was, but, without thinking, I just reached over and picked it up. So, I use paper towels now and forever, even if it turns out to be sock fuzz.

Paper towels are good for wiping up accidents, too. There are many good products on the market now for cleaning and eliminating odor, but paper towels are the first line of defense. If your puppy "goes" on your carpet, get several paper towels and fold them together to make a thick pad. Place it over the spot and step on it, rocking your foot back and forth. Make another pad and repeat the process until you aren't getting up any more moisture. This method effectively blots up a lot of the urine. Next, apply whatever cleaning product

you've chosen, making sure that it is made to eliminate pet odors and stains. In a pinch, use vinegar. Remember, never use ammonia or an ammonia-based product. There's ammonia in urine, and dogs are naturally drawn to the scent and will continue to use that area as their bathroom.

Paper towels are good for wiping off wet or muddy feet or dirty tummies. If you have a taller dog, tummy cleaning might not be an issue, but with my Corgis, spring means they get muddy. You can also use a regular bath towel, but I prefer a towel made from bamboo. It does a good job of cleaning off the mud, and then it easily rinses clean and dries quickly for the next use.

If your dog throws up or has an accident that involves loose stool (I said this was about icky), you may need something more than paper towels. In these cases, I use a plastic dustpan and paper towels to scrape up a mess and get as much of it as possible into the dustpan. Then I can dump the mess into the toilet, easily wash off the dustpan, and clean the floor or carpet. Another solution is to use a couple of paper plates. Fold the plates in half and crease the edge. This sharp edge makes it easy for the plate to go under the goop, and you

Sometimes your dog will just need a good old-fashioned bath.

can use the second plate to push and trap the rest of the mess. If whatever it was has been sitting awhile before you discover it, you may have a stain. I've found that an old toothbrush can make a good little scrub brush. Then you can treat the stain with a carpet cleaner.

There will come a time in the life of your dog when your veterinarian will ask for a stool sample. Stool samples are relatively easy; you just retrieve a piece after your dog has relieved himself. Getting it to the vet's office is more of a challenge. Options include small plastic bags and clean pill bottles (that have not previously held pills). Ask your pharmacist for a couple of clean, unused bottles and keep them in your kitchen junk drawer until you need one. They are small, easy to handle, and have secure lids.

For urine samples, many veterinarians prefer to catheterize the dog so that the urine is not contaminated by outside sources, but if your vet asks you to get a sample, those same unused pill bottles work for carrying the urine. What they don't work for is collecting the urine in the first place. With male dogs, a friend of mine has had good luck using a small paper cup taped to the end of a yardstick or a thin dowel. Many dogs will stop going if you get too close, so the stick allows you to stay back a bit and extend the cup for the collection. With females, form a narrow tray out of aluminum foil that you can quickly slide under your dog. If your dog is skittish about that, tape the foil tray to a yardstick or dowel to give you more distance from your dog.

Everyday Care

A crate is one of the best investments you can make before your puppy comes home. A crate makes housetraining much easier, and it provides a cozy den for your dog. Don't make the mistake of looking at a crate and thinking "cage" or "jail." Dogs are den animals. They appreciate an enclosed space where they feel safe. Think of all the times you've seen a dog curl up under a table or a chair. He is creating his own den.

In addition to providing your dog with a safe spot, a crate makes housetraining easy. No dog will eliminate where he sleeps if he can help it. This doesn't mean that you leave a dog in a crate all day long. The crate is a tool, and, like any tool, it can be abused. Never leave a puppy crated for more than four hours at a time.

Crate your dog:
• when you can't watch him
• at night
• when you're going out
• at mealtimes

Another advantage to using a crate is that if your dog does have an accident, it's in a small, easy-to-clean area, not in the middle of the Oriental carpet.

Crates also make travel safer. Use a crate in your car, and your dog will be protected in an accident. Plus, if your door or window

DID YOU KNOW?

If you've purchased a crate for an adult dog, block off part of the crate with a board so that the large crate doesn't give your puppy a sleeping place at one end and a bathroom place at the other end. Some wire crates come with a partition so that the crate space can grow with the dog.

is broken, your dog won't be able to escape and run away.

Friends and relatives may be more willing to let you visit with your canine pal if they know that your dog will be crated and not running loose, chewing on their furniture.

A motel or hotel that allows pets will likely require that your dog is crated when you are not in your room. An establishment that doesn't ordinarily accept pets may make an exception if the dog is crated while in the room.

Puppies get used to crates quickly, and older dogs can also learn to enjoy the security of a crate, but dogs of all ages need to get used to the crate first. Start by feeding your dog in the crate, with the door open and his food dish just inside the crate door. Tie back the door so that it doesn't accidentally close on your dog. After a few days, move the food dish further back into the crate. Be patient and go slowly. If your dog hesitates or refuses to go into the crate, move the food dish closer to the door. Eventually, your dog will be all the way inside the crate. Close the door while he eats and then open it immediately when he finishes. Gradually leave the door closed for longer and longer amounts of time. If your dog fusses to get out, ignore him until he's quiet and then open the door, praise him, and give him a treat.

Plastic and wire are the main types of crates on the market. If you plan to do much travel by air, invest in a plastic crate that meets airline specifications. Plastic crates are the preferred type for travel; they are cozy, they keep out drafts, and they make your dog feel secure. They also offer better protection in a car in case of an accident.

A WORD OF CAUTION

Some dogs just never get used to an enclosed space. Although a dog might sleep in a crate with the door open, he may panic when the door is shut. Don't force the issue. Let your dog sleep where he's comfortable. Owning a dog is not supposed to be a battle of wills, but a partnership. You need to keep your dog safe and set boundaries, but you also want your dog to be calm and happy.

CRATES FOR SHOWING

If you think you'd like to show your dog, I'd recommend a solid crate because, unfortunately, dogs at shows often lift their legs against just about any surface, including crates. If you have a solid crate, at least your dog and his bedding will stay clean.

A wire crate can fold down for easier transport if you're traveling and will be lugging the crate in and out of motel rooms. A wire crate also offers more ventilation in warm weather. Because wire crates are so open, though, some people buy or make crate covers (or use blankets or towels) to create that cozy den feeling.

Wire crates generally have a removable tray on the bottom, which makes cleaning easier if your dog has an accident in the crate. You can just slide the bottom out, clean it, and put it back. With a plastic crate, you need to either partly crawl into the crate to clean it or remove the top half for easy access.

Your choice of crate boils down to personal preference. I like the solid crates because I use them as bedside tables. There are even designer crates on the market that are designed to look like furniture, made out of wood or covered in an elegant fabric. There's no advantage over a plastic or wire crate except that it will look nicer. If you plan to have a crate in your living room, a designer crate might be your choice. Some professional dog handlers have wooden or metal crates because they're durable and sturdy, but they are also heavier than regular plastic or wire crates.

There are all kinds of dog beds out there, and it can be fun to shop for one for your dog. However, if you get a puppy, you may want to hold off on that designer bed with the inner spring mattress. Your puppy won't know the difference between an old towel and a $200 bed, so, for the first year or so, you might want to stick with towels or an old blanket. You can make the bed comfy with more than one layer, and if you leave the top towel loose, your dog will enjoy scratching and pulling it into a nest. Another advantage is that towels and blankets are easily washable if your puppy has an accident. An alternative might be a thick cotton crib pad, which is highly absorbent but easy to wash and dry.

LARGE-BREED TIP

If you have a large breed, definitely consider a hammock bed or a thick foam bed because the dog's weight, even in a young dog, puts more pressure on the elbows and hips.

Now, let's move to the other end of the age spectrum. Older dogs need more padding than young ones, and they may even have arthritis in their joints. A warm, soft bed will make a senior dog comfortable. For an economical bed, buy a single-bed–sized piece of egg-crate foam. My older dog has a bed in her crate that's two stacked pieces of foam wrapped with towels. The egg-crate foam can be washed gently, and it dries fairly quickly. If you have an old pillow, that would also make a good bed for a small dog, and it recycles the pillow.

When beanbag chairs were popular, my Corgis loved curling up in ours and taking a nap. You can still buy beanbag dog beds; they are soft and warm, and they offer gentle support for older dogs. Any dog can enjoy a beanbag bed, of course. Or, you may want to get a bed filled with shredded foam. Many of these beds have an outer washable cover, and I recommend the ones that have stretched on a frame are excellent for keeping a dog off a cold floor. These beds are popular with large-dog owners because they alleviate any pressure on the dog's joints. Depending on your climate, you might still want to add a blanket or a couple of towels. If you allow your dog on the furniture, or if you let your dog sleep with you, you might not buy a dog bed at all and just let your dog choose where he wants to sleep. Our older Corgi prefers my chair during the day. She can lean on the arm and watch the action outside the window or curl up for a snooze. At night, she prefers stretching out on the loveseat. My chair is protected with towels, and the loveseat is covered entirely by a piece of fleece fabric decorated with paw prints. It was relatively inexpensive and is easy to wash.

a waterproof layer in between the washable cover and filling so that the filling stays dry and clean in case of an accident.

Some beds are just rectangles of solid foam; they are frequently offered in sizes designed to fit crates. Some dog beds are made with inner spring mattresses, giving your dog the same comfort that you enjoy in your bed. Hammock beds or beds made of canvas

DESIGNER BEDS

If you're looking for more style and flair for your dog, there are plenty of designer beds available for as much money as you want to spend. For example, you can get a four-poster bed, complete with a canopy, for your small dog—and for the right price, you can probably find someone to make such a bed for your Mastiff.

Food may seem like a simple matter. The pet-supply store shelves are full of dog foods, and just look at that variety! There are dry foods, canned foods, and semi-moist foods. There are puppy foods, foods for small dogs, foods for seniors, and foods for overweight dogs. There are foods made with beef, chicken, lamb, duck, and fish. You'll need to sift through all of the choices to decide which is best for your dog.

Dry food is the most economical. It is easy to store and may provide some crunching action that can help keep your dog's teeth clean. Dry food will usually contain preservatives. Some dog food companies choose natural, rather than synthetic, preservatives, which include vitamin E (mixed tocopherols), vitamin C (ascorbic acid), and extracts of various plants, such as rosemary.

Canned foods are a favorite with dogs. These foods smell wonderful (to a dog) and are easy to eat. Canned foods cost more than dry foods, and any unused portions must be covered and refrigerated after the can is opened. Because the food is sealed in a can, the canning process itself preserves the food, so canned food does not have preservatives added. Many people stretch their dog food dollar by mixing canned food with dry, making the dry food more palatable.

Semi-moist foods are those foods that usually look most appealing to humans. These foods may look like hamburger patties or beef stew with chunks of vegetables. These foods are the most expensive of the three types. Semi-moist foods, like canned foods, need to be eaten soon after they are opened. They generally contain more flour, sugar, and food colorings than dry or canned foods, but dogs, like people, don't need extra sugar in their diets. Semi-moist foods do have the advantage of being easy to take with you when you travel, and no can opener is necessary.

No matter what kind of food you choose, read the label. Your food should be approved by the American Association of Feed Control Officials (AAFCO), the governing body for all animal feed products, which sets strict guidelines and procedures. For instance, a food may contain "meat by-products," but those by-products may not include feathers, manure, hair, horn, teeth, or hooves. AAFCO regulations mean that whatever is in the food is on the label, and the ingredients must be listed in descending order based on how much of it is in the food.

When you look at a label, you should see a meat protein as the first ingredient listed. Beef, lamb, and chicken are the most common meats but turkey, duck, and venison may also appear. If a food lists "by-products," this may not be all bad. By-products can mean organ meat, such as heart, liver, brain, and intestines, which may sound icky to us but are full of vitamins and minerals. What you want to see, however, are specific by-products, such as beef by-products or chicken by-products, not just "meat"

by-products. Meat by-products could be anything, including zoo animals, roadkill, or animals from animal shelters.

Most dog foods include a filler grain, such as corn, wheat, soy, or rice. Rice is the least likely to cause an allergic reaction. The label will also list preservatives, if any. If you are searching for a preservative-free food, remember that preservatives must be listed only if the manufacturer has added them. The manufacturer may use meat from a source that adds preservatives to the meat, and that will not show up on the label. Remember, too, that AAFCO requirements refer to quantity, not quality, of ingredients. You still have to make the decision on quality.

Another point to consider with food is that not every food is right for every dog. I fed my litter of puppies a premium puppy food that came highly recommended. Three of the puppies did just fine, but the fourth tended to throw up after meals. The food was just too rich for her.

According to the US Food and Drug Administration (FDA), many states require pet food to guarantee the minimum percentages of crude protein and crude fat and the maximum percentages of crude fiber and moisture. Some manufactures include other guarantees as well. What you need to know when comparing nutritional values of dry and canned food is how to convert guarantees to a moisture-free basis. Here's the formula presented by the FDA: find the percentage of whatever you want to measure and find the moisture percentage. Subtract the moisture percentage from 100 to get the dry-weight percentage. Divide the protein (or whatever you're measuring) percentage by the dry-weight percentage and multiply that number by 100. That total is the dry-weight percentage of whatever you are measuring. Generally, canned foods are higher in protein while kibble will have more fiber.

An article on PetEducation.com compares protein sources to determine their quality. Some proteins are better than others. "The ability of a protein to be used by the body

… is summarized as protein quality. Egg has a biological value of 100. Fishmeal and milk … have a value of 92. Beef is around 78 and soybean meal is 67."

The article further suggests that the recommended protein level of a food for puppies should be 28 percent, with 17 percent fat. Adult dogs are fine with 18 percent protein and 9–15 percent fat. Performance dogs are going to need closer to 25 percent protein and 20 percent fat.

Another thing to remember is that the recommended amounts to feed listed on dog food packaging may be excessive. My own dogs would be walking basketballs if I fed the amount suggested on the package. I feed less than half the recommended quantity. It will be trial and error with your own dog, but watch your dog's weight and adjust the food amount accordingly. You should always be able to feel your dog's ribs, but if you can see them, the dog is probably too thin. If you can't feel anything, it's diet time.

56 Other Types of Food

The aforementioned types of commercial dog food offer convenience and a balanced diet. They are consistent in terms of percentages of ingredients and have been tested in food trials. They are relatively easy to store and are generally readily available from pet-supply stores and even grocery stores. However, some other types of dog diets are becoming popular, too. There are freeze-dried, fresh or frozen, and raw foods available commercially. While specialty pet stores may have these, sometimes you have to order online, and, for the most part, they are more expensive.

Freeze-dried foods, cooked and raw, are available at some pet-supply stores and from online retailers. You rehydrate them by mixing them with water. Some must be mixed with a protein, generally cooked or raw meat. Freeze-dried foods have a long shelf life and are lightweight. Because they are freeze-dried, they contain no preservatives.

Frozen foods are often shaped into long rolls, like sausages. You just cut off the needed portion, thaw, and feed. These are not as convenient if you're traveling, but they can last a long time in your freezer.

Some people, though, prefer to cook for their dogs. They like knowing where their dogs' food comes from, and they may purchase only organic products for their dogs. Home cooking does not mean just scraping leftovers into a bowl for your dog. You need to consider the proper balance of protein, fat, fiber, vitamins, and minerals. Dogs, for instance, need more fat in their diet than humans do.

Furthermore, some human foods are hard for dogs to digest; others can cause illness or even death. For example, raw vegetables and fruits take a long time for dogs to digest. Cooked eggs are fine, but a protein in raw egg whites can interfere with biotin, which is essential for the growth of cells, metabolism of fat, and transference of carbon dioxide. Onions can cause hemolytic anemia.

There are other human foods that are not good for dogs. You might not intentionally feed them to your dog, but you need to be careful that your dog can't reach them and that everyone in the family knows that these foods are forbidden for Fido.

Many people feel that the best way to feed a dog is to give raw food. You'll often hear this referred to as the BARF diet, which stands for either Bones And Raw Food or Biologically Appropriate Raw Food. Be warned that no one seems to be neutral on this topic. People who feed raw food will boast of their dogs' shiny coats and white teeth, while opponents warn of bacterial contamination.

Some veterinarians are in favor of feeding raw and some are against it. If you find a terrific veterinarian, and you want to feed raw but he has reservations, suggest that you bring your dog in for a blood test every six months to make sure that all levels are as they should be.

Feeding raw does not mean just throwing down a chunk of meat, either. Once again, you need to be aware of the proper balance of protein, fat, and carbohydrates. Most people who feed raw combine raw meaty bones with organ meat and a vegetable/grain mixture.

Offering fresh raw bones is an important part of feeding a raw diet. Recreational chewing is fine, but you must dispose of raw bones after two or three days, when the bone dries out and can be just as dangerous as a cooked bone. To avoid potential problems, some people grind all bones before offering them to their dogs.

There are excellent books dedicated to the subject of feeding raw. These informative volumes can guide you regarding how much to feed your dog and the correct proportions of the various nutrients for proper balance.

57 When, Where, and How to Feed?

When to Feed?

How many times a day you feed your dog may depend on the size of your dog as well as his age. Large and giant dogs should eat two or even three times a day rather than one big meal to help prevent bloat. Young puppies need to be fed up to four times a day, and senior dogs may do better if they are fed twice a day. Medium and small dogs who are not prone to bloat may be fed once a day, but your personal preference and schedule factor into your dog's feeding schedule.

I feed my Corgis twice a day because when I got my first Corgi, I also had a large mixed-breed who was fed twice a day. It just made sense to feed all of the dogs together at the same time, and I've just kept the same schedule with all of my dogs.

Free feeding is another option. Some people like to just fill up a bowl and let the dog munch on and off whenever he is hungry. There are drawbacks to this system, one of which is that, unless you monitor how much your dog is eating, he can easily become overweight. If you're feeding more than one dog, you won't know which dog is getting the majority of the food. Also, that ever-present bowl of

> **COOKING TIPS**
> If you decide to cook for your dog, cook up a large batch of food and then freeze it in meal-sized portions. If you board your dog, make sure that the kennel has enough room in a refrigerator or freezer for your dog's food. If you travel with your dog, you'll have to make sure that you can keep the food chilled while you're en route.

food might lead to aggression between dogs. Additionally, the time might come when one of your dogs needs a different kind of food, and you need to be sure that he's the one eating it. Even if you have just one dog, you'll be limited to feeding dry food only because canned or semi-moist food will spoil if left out all day.

Where to Feed?

Dogs, of course, don't care where they're fed. They just want the food. Many people find the kitchen a convenient place. Some people like to feed their dogs outdoors. If you've decided to feed raw, you might want those raw bones to be gnawed outside. If that's your choice, be careful that you don't leave uneaten food out because it could attract unwanted wildlife.

Multiple dogs may mean separate dining areas. My current dogs are fine eating together in the kitchen, but it was not always that way. At one time, I fed one dog in a crate, one dog in the mudroom, one in the kitchen, and one in my office. At other times, depending on how many crates were in the kitchen, they were all crated for meals. You don't want dogs to get in an argument over food or to have a pushy dog hog all the food.

Bowls

There are all kinds of dog bowls on the market, and many are decorated with adorable designs, but look beyond the artwork. Your three basic choices are plastic, ceramic, and stainless steel.

Plastic dishes may be the cheapest. They are lightweight and don't easily break. They come in many colors, and most are dishwasher safe. Plastic, however, can be inviting for a dog to chew on, and the resulting scratches can harbor harmful bacteria. In short-nosed breeds, a chin rubbing on plastic can lead to a case of canine acne. If a plastic dish is not dishwasher safe, it can be very hard to thoroughly clean. If you have decided to feed raw, cross plastic off your list of dish choices.

Ceramic dishes are heavy and can't easily be shoved around the room. They can break, though. If you choose ceramic, make sure that the paint or glaze is lead-free.

Stainless steel is almost indestructible. It is lightweight, easy to clean, and nonporous. It comes in a wide variety of shapes and sizes, and many types have a rubber ring on the bottom to help keep the bowl in one spot.

Water

No matter what kind of food you feed or how often or in what kind of bowl, your dog should always have access to clean water in a clean bowl. Water is essential, and if you and your dog are out in the yard in the summer, make sure there's a bowl of water outdoors as well as inside.

58 Does a Dog Need Variety?

The prevailing thought for years was that once you found a food that worked for your dog, you stuck with the same diet and fed it consistently. It's still true that if your dog has been eating the same food for a long time, any changes should be made gradually, over several days to a week.

To switch your dog to a new food, mix a little of the new in with the old, gradually increasing the ratio of new to old until the dog's entire portion is the new food. When a dog's digestive system is used to a particular food, his intestinal bacteria has adapted to processing that food. If you suddenly add something new to the food, the bacteria don't know what to do with it. If you have vegetarian friends, they will likely tell you that eating meat now makes them sick because they can no longer properly process it. Many people feel that dogs should be fed a variety of different foods. If you have chosen to feed raw or are cooking for your dog, he will be getting variety. If you choose to feed a commercial food, you may want to mix it up by rotating several different brands, but there's no proof that this is a better way to feed your dog. If you feed the same food all the time, and your dog is doing well on that food, that's fine, too.

There are many types of treats for dogs on the market, and many dogs eat occasional tidbits of "people food" as well. Treats, regardless of what type you feed, should make up no more 10 percent of your dog's total diet. If your dog seems to be gaining weight, the first place to cut back is treats.

It's fun to give dogs treats, and food rewards are a great way to train, but try to use quality treats. Many soft dog treats are basically flour and sugar. It would be better to cook up some liver and cut it into small pieces. You can also buy freeze-dried liver. If you're training your dog and using food rewards, offer very small pieces, no matter the size of the dog. Break hard dog biscuits into pieces or buy small-sized biscuits.

Dogs enjoy bones to gnaw on, but only fresh, raw—never cooked—bones. If you do give your dog a bone, make sure it's appropriate to his size; always go bigger rather than smaller. You don't want your dog to swallow a small bone and have it get stuck in his throat. Throw the bone away after two or three days because, by then, even a raw bone can splinter and crack into dangerous pieces.

Rawhide chew toys are popular, but be very careful. If you have a Bulldog, for instance, never give him rawhide. Bulldogs tend to swallow large chunks, which can lead to impacted bowels. Pressed rawhide is a safer alternative. If you choose to give your dog rawhide, check the labels and use products made in the United States because you'll run less risk of the product's having been manufactured with arsenic.

Cow hooves were popular chews for a while, but they stained my carpet and tended to smell bad. Anything smoked may also stain furniture or carpet.

I try to find single-ingredient treats; if those ingredients are human-grade, I'm even happier. My dogs love dried sweet potato, and I like knowing that it's completely digestible and has no added chemicals.

Some people absolutely never give their dog any leftovers and never toss their dog a bite of sandwich or a handful of popcorn. I am not one of those people. Life's too short, and it's too much fun to share with my dogs. I have never fed any of our dogs from the table, but I will put a spoonful of leftover mashed potatoes in their bowls. If we've eaten something with gravy, the dogs get to lick the plates. If we're enjoying some popcorn in the evening, it's fun to toss pieces and see if the dogs can catch them. Pizza night means that the dogs get a bite of the crust.

We don't give any treats in excess, and we're selective about what we give. I'm happy to add a bit of salmon or haddock to their food bowls if we bring home a doggy bag; if it's fried fish, I take off all of the the coating and give the dogs just the fish. At Thanksgiving, they may get a bit of turkey, but never spicy stuffing and never too much gravy. Green beans are a good additive if you're trying to help your dog lose weight. They're low-cal and help to fill your dog up. A spoonful of pumpkin is tasty and is loaded with vitamins. The key word here is "pumpkin." Don't give your dog pumpkin pie filling. My dogs never get pie, cake, cookies, or candy.

It's your decision about whether or not to offer the occasional bit of cheese or some leftover egg. If you decide it's OK, remember that dogs are creatures of habit, and it doesn't take long for them to learn new rules. After giving our dogs a bite of cheese at lunchtime for a couple of days in a row, it became a ritual. No matter what kind of sandwich we're making, the dogs come running for their cheese. It doesn't hurt them, and we don't mind, but I am glad that we didn't offer them filet mignon.

59 Recipes

For those who enjoy cooking for their dogs, here are a few easy recipes for treats that you and your pal can share.

Muffie's Muffins

Ingredients
- 2½ cups cornmeal
- 1½ cups flour
- 2 tablespoons vegetable oil
- 1 egg
- ⅔ cup honey
- ½ teaspoon baking powder
- ½ teaspoon cinnamon
- ½ teaspoon nutmeg
- 1 ⅓ cups water
- ½ cup rolled oats (optional)

Preheat oven to 350 degrees F.

Mix all ingredients but the oats in a large bowl. Line a muffin tin with paper baking cups. Pour the batter into the cups and sprinkle with the rolled oats. Bake for 40 minutes.

Biscuits for Bowser

Ingredients
- 1 tablespoon baking powder
- 1 egg
- 1 cup smooth or crunchy peanut butter
- 2½ cups whole wheat flour (or any flour you prefer)
- ¾ cup nonfat milk

Preheat oven to 325 degrees F.

In a large mixing bowl, beat together the milk, egg, and peanut butter. Add in the flour and baking powder to make a very stiff dough, using your hands to work in the last of the flour if necessary.

Flour a work surface and roll out the dough to a ¼ -inch thickness. Cut into desired sizes depending on the size of your dog. If you don't have cookie cutters, use the rim of a glass dipped in flour or just use a knife to cut squares or rectangles.

Bake on a parchment-lined baking sheet for 20 minutes. Turn biscuits over and bake for an additional 15 minutes.

Remove from oven and allow to cool completely before storing in an airtight container.

Cool Treats for Canines

None of these measurements is exact. If you can't buy a 16-ounce container of yogurt, for instance, use 12 ounces and maybe a bit less peanut butter. If you don't have a banana, mash up some strawberries or stir in some blueberries. If your dog doesn't like peanut butter (highly unlikely), just freeze the yogurt-fruit mixture. No honey? Leave it out.

Ingredients
- 1 ripe banana
- 1 cup peanut butter
- 2 cups plain yogurt
- 2 tablespoons honey

Mash the banana and stir into the yogurt. Warm the peanut butter in the microwave until it's easy to stir. Add the banana/yogurt mixture and the honey to the softened peanut butter. Mix all of the ingredients together, pour the mixture into ice-cube trays, and freeze overnight.

60 Collars

Even with a completely fenced yard, your dog will need a collar or harness. It's nice to be able to take your dog for a walk now and then, and it's a good way to help socialize a puppy. Beyond that, there are times when you need to get your dog from one point to the other, whether to the vet's office, the groomer, or a boarding kennel. You also need a collar to hold your dog's license and rabies tags.

Initially, buy a simple adjustable buckle collar. Puppies grow fast, and, depending on the breed, you might go through three or four collars before your dog reaches adult size. You might even consider buying a cat collar for a puppy. There are also nylon collars that don't have holes; the tongue of the buckle pushes right through the fabric, making it easy to fit the collar to your puppy as he grows. Even puppies of strong breeds like the American Pit Bull Terrier don't need anything heavier. I once saw a very young pit bull puppy with three loops of chain around his neck. It's unnecessary and looks ridiculous.

Once your dog is an adult, you can think about a permanent collar that may add a touch of pizzazz. Leather collars are more expensive, but they will likely last the life of your dog. There are flat and rolled leather collars; the latter are narrower and will prevent matting down the fur. If you plan to show your dog, and he has a longer coat, this might be your preferred collar.

Choke collars are not recommended for training or walking your dog.

Nylon is also a good choice. It's strong and long lasting, and it comes in many different colors and designs. You can usually get a leash in a matching color or pattern.

Another popular style is the martingale collar, which, like a training collar, can tighten around the dog's throat, but, unlike a training collar, it can only tighten so much. Martingale collars are made of two loops. The larger loop goes around your dog's neck, and the smaller loop connects the ends of the larger loop and can be used to tighten the larger loop. A dog who can easily pull out of a plain buckle collar will have more trouble getting out of a martingale collar. These collars are sometimes called "Greyhound collars" because they are frequently used with sighthounds. If you have a sighthound, you might be able to find a wide, beautifully embroidered one and really make a fashion statement.

If you've decided to try showing in conformation, you'll

need a show collar, which is a thinner, lighter version of a martingale collar. It is designed to control the dog but be almost invisible, therefore not ruining the neckline of the dog and letting the judge concentrate on the dog without being distracted by a collar or lead.

Another collar, used in the sport of coursing, is the slip collar. These are not meant for walking a dog, but are used as quick-release collars for coursing. They are very wide and made of leather or fabric. They have two large rings at each end, and the leash is fastened to the collar. By drawing part of the leash through the loops, a handler can easily release a coursing hound by just letting go of one end.

Training collars, often called "choke collars," are going out of fashion, and that's not a bad thing. Used for training, they tighten around

HARNESS DIFFERENCES
Remember that a harness that you might use to walk your dog or for tracking is not the same as a harness that a dog uses to pull. If you think you'd like to try a dog sport such as weight pulling, carting, mushing, or skijoring, talk to people in the sport and make sure you get the proper type of harness.

the dog's neck when the "live" ring is pulled. If you use this type of collar and leave it on your dog all the time, you run the risk of that "live" ring catching on something and choking your dog. Years ago, I was walking my 110-pound dog Ginger on a training collar. We stopped at a neighbor's house, and she asked me to tie my dog on the deck. Fortunately, I knew enough to transfer the

A show collar and lead are thin and lightweight.

MUZZLES

Some communities have laws requiring any "pit-bull-type" dog to wear a muzzle when out in public. If you've chosen one of the bully breeds and you live in such a community, get a basket muzzle that allows your dog to breathe normally. Basket muzzles also allow your dog to pant and to drink water.

Nylon muzzles that fit snugly over the dog's snout are for temporarily restraining a dog at the vet's office or grooming salon. A dog should never wear one of these muzzles for a long period of time.

leash to Ginger's buckle collar because she fell off the deck steps, 10 feet from the ground. The collar pulled off over her head, and she was fine. Had I left the leash attached to the training collar, I'd have had a dead dog. If you feel you must use a training collar, never, ever leave it on your dog unattended.

Instead of a collar, another option is a head halter. You can't easily use these on short-nosed breeds, like the Bulldog, but they can be a good option for other dogs. With a head halter, one loop goes over the dog's head, right behind the ears, and another loop goes over the muzzle. The muzzle loop has a ring on the underside, and that's where you attach the lead. The dog is controlled by your turning his head rather than tugging on his neck. Head halters eliminate neck injuries and can help in teaching a dog to walk nicely on a slack lead. A head halter is not a muzzle. The loop over the dog's muzzle is loose and is far enough back on the dog's face that he can eat, drink, and pant with no obstruction.

You may prefer a harness, which leaves the dog's head totally free, with no pressure on the neck at all. A harness may work better with smaller breeds because you have less control over your dog with a harness, and a harness may encourage your dog to pull. There are also harnesses to which you fasten the lead to a ring at the dog's chest. With this type of harness, a dog who forges ahead will turn back to face you with a tug on the lead.

Whatever kind of collar or harness you decide to use, if your dog wears it all the time, remember to give it a good cleaning periodically. Imagine how dirty your shirt collar would become if you never washed your shirt. Leather collars can be cleaned with saddle soap. Nylon collars will come clean using a bit of shampoo with an old toothbrush as a scrub brush, or you can tie a nylon collar in a sock and throw it in your washing machine.

A head halter, shown, does not obstruct the dog like a muzzle does.

There are many types and sizes of leashes (or leads—the terms are synonymous) in many different materials. Cheap plastic is just that, so don't bother. It may look like leather initially, and the price may tempt you, but resist. It will crack and be stiff in your hand. Also steer away from chain leads. No matter how large and powerful your dog is, a good leather or nylon lead will be just as effective, and you have less control with a chain lead unless you plan to wear gloves all the time. It's hard to gather up a chain lead if you want to shorten it, and, should your dog suddenly lunge forward, that chain will rip across the palm of your hand.

For everyday use, choose a 4- or 6-foot nylon or leather lead. It doesn't have to be particularly wide, either. You can get nylon leads in assorted colors and patterns, and it can be nice to match your dog's collar and lead. I prefer a 6-foot lead because it gives your dog a little leeway to meander and sniff as you go along. Also, I have short dogs, so 4 feet wouldn't give me much extra length.

I also love leather leads. Leather will cost more to begin with, but it will last a long time, especially if you get one with an end braided through the clasp instead of stitched. The leather will get softer and more supple with use. I even have two very thin, fine leather show leads.

If you're tracking with your dog, you'll need a long line of nylon or cotton, 20 to 40 feet in length. Occasionally, when we're traveling, if we're in an open area, I like to have my dogs on something longer than the 6-foot leash. That's when this kind of long line works well. I created my own with cotton clothesline that I tied to a clasp I bought at the hardware store. It's not elegant; in fact, it's pretty tacky, and I would never take it onto a tracking trail, but it's fine for once or twice a year.

A very common lead, which is frequently misused, is the flexible lead that retracts

into a plastic handle. Most people don't know how to use this type of lead properly, and they give their dog 15 feet of freedom, which can be too much, depending on the setting and the dog. There is a brake on the plastic handle, so, in theory, you can shorten the lead by pulling up and back and then applying the brake, but too many people seem not to know how to do this.

Retractable leads are frequently banned from show sites. A dog on a 15-foot lead can easily get far enough ahead to get out into a road and get hit by a car if the owner isn't paying strict attention. In an emergency, if you need to grab the lead, you are grabbing a thin nylon cord that can burn your palms when the dog leaps forward. I once helped a woman who had two Shih Tzus, each on a flexible lead. The dogs each had 15 feet of freedom and had already tripped the lady's husband, who was on crutches. The only way I could help was to grasp the leads much closer to the dogs. It's not comfortable hanging onto those nylon cords. I did suggest that she get regular leads.

If you're out in the open, a flexible lead can be a wonderful way to let your dog have

some freedom while still keeping him under control, but in crowded places, or even out for a walk around the block, a regular lead is much better and safer.

Another kind of lead is a slip lead, or a kennel lead. This is a collar and leash all in one, with a loop that slides over the dog's head; the loop is pulled tight by the part that forms the lead. It's not for everyday walking, but is useful for short distances. For instance, many kennels or veterinary offices will use a kennel lead to move your dog to a run or a cage. If your dog is in the yard and is too interested in squirrels to come inside when you call, a kennel lead makes it easy to get your dog and lead him to the house.

Flexible lead

All dogs need exercise, some more than others. If you have a Chihuahua, he may get all the exercise he needs from following you around the house and enjoying the occasional game of fetch or hide-and-seek. If you have a Dalmatian, he will need plenty of exercise, including long walks and opportunities to do some running. If you enjoy jogging, a Dalmatian will be your happy companion.

Walks may be your dog's only form of exercise. If you'll be walking on sidewalks, you'll get the added benefit that the cement will help wear down your dog's nails. Small and medium-sized dogs won't need as many walks as larger dogs. A Corgi, for instance, will be happy with a mile-long walk and some shorter ones throughout the day.

If all of your dog's exercise will be on lead, it will be more pleasant for you both if he will walk on a loose lead without constantly lunging and pulling. This does not mean that your dog always has to walk in the heel position. It's wonderful if your dog is well trained and will heel, but if walks are his sole outings, let him wander a bit. Let him enjoy the smells of squirrels, cats, and other dogs. When we lived in Arizona, our dogs were always on lead, but if they saw a rabbit, we always ran with them as they chased it.

Fenced-in yards are wonderful for both you and your dog. They are especially nice

OBSTACLE COURSE

Set up your own obstacle course for your dog, along the lines of an agility course, with some jumps, a low see-saw, and inexpensive tunnels.

for those early-morning and late-night potty breaks when you can let your dog out while you stay warm inside the house. However, having a fenced yard doesn't mean that your dog won't still need exercise. You'll need to get out there, too, and throw a ball or play some other game that gets your dog moving. Indoors or out, playing with your dog is good for both of you.

If you have a terrier, you might consider choosing a special area of the yard where your dog can dig. An easy way to create a digging pit is to get a child's wading pool and fill it with dirt or sand. Encourage your dog to dig in this spot, not in the yard, by lightly burying treats. Once your dog gets the idea, bury toys or more treats and let him use his instincts to unearth the treasures. And speaking of wading pools, many dogs enjoy splashing in these shallow pools in the summer.

Dog parks can be great places for your dog to burn off some energy and just be a dog, but you need to pay attention to the different rules of each dog park. All dog parks are not the same. Each park will have a list of rules, usually posted on the gate, and, if you're lucky, the people using the park will follow those rules. There's also park etiquette to consider, which means having common courtesy toward the other people and dogs in the park.

No matter the dog park, the rules will include picking up after your dog. This is not optional. Pay attention to your dog and clean up immediately before other dogs or humans step in it and before it starts to draw flies. If the park doesn't supply cleanup bags, make sure to bring enough with you. Take a few extra in case someone else runs out.

Many parks restrict their use to dogs that are spayed and neutered. Respect that rule; it's to help prevent aggression between dogs. Also make sure that your dog is current on all vaccinations. If your dog is ill, don't take him to the park and spread germs.

If you're looking for a dog park, try to find one that has separate areas for small and large dogs. Dog parks should be fun, and it's not fun for a small dog to be intimidated by larger dogs.

Also look for a park with an "airlock"—a smaller, gated area where people enter and exit the park. This can prevent loose dogs from escaping when someone goes in or out. If you

EXERCISE OPTIONS

If your dog doesn't make friends with other dogs easily, try to find a dog walker or dog sitter who will come to your house while you're at work to spend some time playing fetch with him or taking him for a brisk walk.

are already in the park and someone new is arriving, keep your dog from rushing the gate and allow the newcomer to enter safely.

Many parks have a water tap and may even have a bowl or two. It's a good idea to carry your own bowl to help prevent the spread of germs. You can carry your own water for your dog if you like, but never take food to the park for you or for your dog. You don't want to cause a fight because several dogs all want the same tasty treat. The same may apply to toys. If another dog tries to play with your dog's favorite toy, your dog could become territorial over his property.

Watch your dog at all times and be an advocate for your dog. It's easy to start chatting with a friend and not watch your dog, but it's important that you know where your dog is at all times. If your dog is large and playful, control him if he is overwhelming or frightening another dog. Conversely, don't let other dogs bully your dog. If you see a situation that might lead to a fight, or if your dog looks unhappy, remove your dog immediately. Don't wait for the other

owner to act first, and don't wait to see if the situation will resolve itself.

Don't have an "I was here first" or a "he started it" mentality. It's your responsibility to keep your dog safe. If you know that your dog doesn't get along with a particular dog, go to the park when the other dog is not there. If that dog arrives, leave. If that dog is already at the park, go home. Always be willing to redirect your dog's attention or to leash your dog for a while if play is getting out of hand.

Train your dog to come when you call, no matter the distraction. This can interrupt a potential fight, and it's faster than trying to reach your dog before trouble starts. You are responsible for your dog. It's up to you to protect him and also to keep him from threatening or annoying any other dogs.

Doggy daycare can provide a way for your dog to get some socialization and exercise while you're at work, but you won't be there to watch your dog and to remove him

if there's a problem. Daycare for dogs will have similar rules as dog parks concerning up-to-date shots and may take only spayed and neutered animals. See if the facility has a separate area for smaller dogs. What provisions are made for dogs if they need a time-out or to rest by themselves? Some kennels offer daycare, giving each dog his own run and allowing specified playtimes with other dogs in a larger area. If your dog will be playing with other dogs, see if you can observe the play for a while so you can tell how well your dog will do in this setting.

Once your dog has gotten used to the daycare environment, he should be eager to enter when you bring him there. If he's dragging his feet, maybe it's not his favorite place. It's important for your dog to get exercise, but it's also important that your dog is happy and is not in danger. Use good judgment in choosing a dog park or doggy daycare.

Whether you have a short-coated dog who requires very little grooming or an Old English Sheepdog who needs extensive brushing every day, you'll need some basic grooming supplies.

Bathing

First, no matter what kind of dog you have, stock up on old towels. Yard sales are good places to find usable, inexpensive towels. Ask friends and relatives to check their linen closets for worn-out towels that they're willing to donate. Towels are useful in all kinds of ways, from wiping muddy feet to covering furniture to sopping up water if you have a puppy who thinks his water bowl is a pool. When you give your dog a bath, you'll need more towels than you think.

Speaking of baths, if your dog is small enough and you have a stationary laundry tub, that's a good place for a bath. You won't have to bend over that far, so your back and knees won't suffer too much. If you don't have such a tub, or you have a larger dog, you'll need to use your own bathtub.

Before you start running the water, get a small pillow for your knees. Put a rubber mat in the bottom of the tub so that your dog won't slip. If you have a shower attachment, you can use that for washing your dog. Otherwise, buy a special sprayer attachment for the faucet at a pet-supply store. This will allow you to reach your dog with the spray end of the attachment. Alternatively, you can just use water from the tap and a pitcher or other container to wet and rinse your dog, but that takes much

BEFORE YOU BATHE
If you have a short-coated dog, he can go right into the bath, but for a dog with any kind of a coat, brush him thoroughly before the bath. If you don't remove all tangles and mats before wetting the coat, the water will just make them worse.

longer and makes it harder to get all of the soap out of your dog's coat.

Use a shampoo especially formulated for dogs. "People shampoo" will dry out your dog's coat and skin. Use lukewarm water and wet your dog thoroughly from the neck back. Try not to get water in your dog's ears. You can put a cotton ball in each ear to prevent water from entering, but in my experience, your dog will just shake his head until the cotton comes out. Use a wet washcloth, without soap, to wipe off your dog's muzzle and head.

Lather up the shampoo on your dog's body and squeeze it through his coat. Don't scrub—that will just tangle the coat. Rinse and repeat.

Make sure that you rinse thoroughly, paying special attention to the feet and behind the elbows. Once you've finished, if you're lucky, your dog will shake while he's still in the tub. Otherwise, quickly wrap him in a towel and try to towel off as much water as you can before he shakes. Lift or help him from the tub. Don't let him scramble out on his own because he may injure himself.

If you're giving a bath in the summer, you can just let your dog air-dry. If it's cold out, or if you have a dog with a very heavy coat, you'll need to use a hair dryer. If you have a dog with a heavy coat, and you'll be giving him baths regularly, invest in a hair dryer especially for dogs. If you use your own hair dryer, always use it on the lowest setting and keep it moving over the dog.

Brushing

While you may not need to bathe your smooth-coated dog very often, he will benefit from regular brushing. Consider using a hound glove. This is a glove covered with little round nubs that help get rid of loose, dead hair and dandruff. During shedding season, you can use a small rubber brush similar to a horse's currycomb. Finish by brushing your dog with a soft-bristle brush; you can use a human baby's brush if your dog is small. A baby brush is also good for brushing the feet, which tend to be more sensitive than the rest of the body.

For dogs with long fur, the currycomb-type brush is good for removing dead guard hairs. Use long strokes, brushing in the direction of the fur. If your dog is shedding and has a thick undercoat, you'll want a special brush, sometimes called a grooming rake or shedding blade, that grabs a lot of the loose undercoat.

For regular grooming, whether every day or once a week, a slicker brush works well on dogs with an undercoat. A slicker brush has thin wire bristles set at an angle. Brush small sections of coat at a time, pushing the fur back against the grain with your hand and then using the slicker brush to gradually brush the fur out from under your hand. Spraying the coat with a light mist of water helps prevent the individual hairs from breaking and helps control static electricity.

A pin brush, as its name implies, looks like someone stuck a bunch of straight pins into the rubber bed of the brush. The ends left sticking up are rounded into small balls so that the pins don't scratch the dog. A pin brush is useful for detangling coats, especially on dogs like setters.

Use a comb to quickly run through the coat and to work on small tangles. Combs come with various numbers of teeth per inch. A flea comb is a very fine-toothed comb that can trap fleas as you comb.

If you have a Poodle, a Bichon Frise, or any breed with curly hair that needs constant trimming, and you decide to groom the dog yourself rather than make regular trips to the groomer, you'll need clippers. If you don't know how to use them, ask for advice from someone with experience so that your clip is an even length and you don't cut your dog's skin.

Scissors are a useful tool when grooming any dog. If you're trimming your dog's hair, you may want to scissor hard-to-reach areas or use the scissors to give a cleaner look to where you've clipped. You can also use scissors to trim fur around the pads of your dog's feet. With Poodles and some other breeds with drop ears, you may also want hemostats for plucking hair from the ear.

65 Nail Care

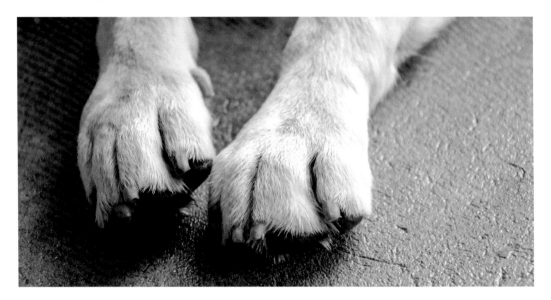

Another part of grooming your dog is cutting his nails. If you're planning to show your dog, you'll want to trim them frequently, and most pet dogs will probably need a trim at least once a month. If you walk your dog almost exclusively on a sidewalk, his nails may be worn down naturally, and you may never need to trim them.

Neglected nails can make it hard for your dog to walk, and they also tend to pull the toes away from each other, giving your dog a splayfoot that is not only unattractive but can interfere with proper movement. Long nails can also catch and break. This is painful, and the broken nail may bleed and get infected.

Nail cutting is painless when done properly, but many dogs dislike having their feet handled. If you get a puppy, touch and rub each foot at least once every day. Get him used to someone touching his feet as a youngster, and it may make nail cutting more pleasant for both of you.

When you cut your dog's nails, avoid the quick, which is the dark blood vessel running through the middle of the nail. If your dog has white nails, you'll be able to see the quick; if the nails are black, you won't, but if you cut the nail just where it starts to curve, you should be OK. If you accidentally cut the

GRINDER TIP
If you decide to use a grinder to trim your dog's nails, don't just hold the wheel against the nail—move it around the nail and stop at intervals to let the heat dissipate.

quick, use a touch of styptic powder to stop the bleeding or just hold your finger tightly to the end of the nail until the bleeding stops.

There are different tools for cutting nails, and your choice of tool is a matter of personal preference.

- A grinder, or Dremel tool, is an electric or battery-powered tool with a rapidly rotating abrasive head. This head wears down the nail.
- Nail scissors are good for smaller dogs. They look like safety scissors.

- Pliers-style cutters are heavier duty than scissors and are good for medium and large dogs.
- The guillotine-type trimmer has a sharp blade that slices through the nail.

If you find that you don't like clipping your dog's nails or that your dog dislikes it so much that it's a chore for both of you, find a local groomer to do it. Whatever method you choose, just make sure that your dog's nails stay short and comfortable.

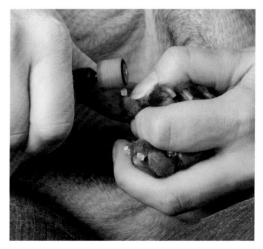

One of the best things about your new dog is that you will have a playmate, ready for a game anytime you are. Use your imagination, and your dog will happily join you in whatever game you can think of.

Playing fetch with a tennis ball is fun for many medium and large dogs, and tennis balls are relatively inexpensive. A tennis ball that is no longer good for human play is still just fine for a dog. Many pet-supply companies make rubber balls that also work well. Stay away from baseballs and softballs because they can really hurt if you accidentally hit your dog with one. My dog Gael loves to play fetch and frequently starts running before I throw the ball. One day, I accidentally hit her in the face. She was able to shake it off, and there was no permanent damage. I hate to think what might have happened to her eye had she been hit by a baseball.

If your dog loves to retrieve, you might find a ball launcher useful; this is a long plastic arm that helps you throw the ball farther while saving your own arm from the strain of repetitive throwing. Another benefit: when the ball gets coated in saliva, you can pick it up with the ball launcher and avoid getting slimy hands.

Some dogs ignore balls but love a good game of tug-of-war, and there are some wonderful tug toys available. Some people feel that this kind of game encourages aggression, but if you set the ground rules and are observant, you can enjoy a game of tug with your pet. If things get too wild, just drop your end of the toy and let your dog win. Letting your dog win doesn't mean that you're letting him become the boss; it simply means that, at that moment, he gets the toy.

You can also play games that make your dog think. Set up simple challenges for your dog with just a few household items. For instance, take a muffin tin and several balls that fill the cup holes but are large enough so that your dog can easily remove them. Put

a dog treat under each ball and then set the pan down and watch your dog figure out how to get at the treats. You can play the same sort of game with three paper or plastic cups and treats. You can either hide a treat under each cup (don't let your dog see you doing it) or hide just one treat and let your dog choose the correct cup.

In another version of this game, you go into a room without your dog, hide a treat, and

then let him find it. Start simple, with the treat in plain sight on the floor, and gradually move on to putting it up on a chair or under a sheet of newspaper. If you're playing outdoors, hide treats under a shrub or under some leaves.

You can play games with your dog and practice obedience commands at the same time. Hide-and-seek is a game that dogs seem to enjoy. Have your dog sit and stay or just have someone hold your dog while you run and hide. Holler your release word (such as "OK") or ask the person holding your dog to release him. The first few times you play, just hide in another room, but in sight. Once your dog understands the game, hide behind a door, under a bed, or in a closet, as long as the door is ajar and your dog can get to you. You can play this game outdoors, too, if your yard has trees or bushes to hide behind.

67 Playing by Himself

Dogs enjoy playing alone, too, and there are hundreds of dog toys on the market that your dog can enjoy by himself. When buying toys for your dog, be sure to get size-appropriate toys; when in doubt, buy bigger rather than smaller. Small toys can choke a larger dog, and a stronger dog's jaws might break a toy made for a smaller dog, creating dangerous pieces that might cut him or, if swallowed, cause internal injury.

Stuffed toys are almost always a canine favorite. Some dogs will carry their favorite stuffed toy everywhere, and a puppy may just cuddle with a stuffed toy, treating it like a littermate. Other dogs consider it an accomplishment to disembowel a stuffed toy as quickly as possible. Almost all my Corgis have gone for the "kill," searching for the squeaker in the center of the toy and ripping and tearing until they find it. If your dog likes to do this, supervise his play and be prepared to dig out and remove

SQUEAKY TOYS

Be cautious with any type of toy that contains a squeaker because many dogs try to "desqueak" their toys and may even try to eat the squeaker.

If the noise of a squeaky toy annoys you, look for toys with noisemakers that emit sounds only dogs can hear. Your dog will still treat it like any other stuffed toy, but you won't hear it.

wads of stuffing so that your dog doesn't ingest it. Don't let your dog keep the squeaky part, either, because he could easily swallow it. Once the noisemaker is "dead" and no longer squeaks, don't be surprised if your dog then ignores the toy.

Nylon chew toys are popular and can provide good jaw exercise. Generally, dogs can't break or chew off large portions; rather, they scrape small bits of nylon off the toy, which pass harmlessly through the dog's system. Buy an appropriate size because you don't want your dog to be able to swallow the toy whole. My dogs have always loved these nylon toys, but they have, on occasion, broken a tooth, which has had to be pulled. I still consider them safer and less messy than real bones, though.

My dogs have never had much interest in hard rubber toys to chew on, but if your dog likes that type, there's not

Fill a toy with peanut butter or cheese to hold your dog's interest.

much chance of a broken tooth. Some hard rubber toys also have a place to hide food items, like peanut butter or cheese. Dogs will spend a long time with this type of toy, and you can give this type of toy to your dog when you're leaving the house to keep him occupied. Before leaving your dog with any toy, though, make sure you know how your dog will act with it. A dog with very strong jaws could gnaw off large chunks of a rubber toy, and you don't want him to swallow those chunks.

Another type of toy dispenses food treats; it can be as simple as a ball or box with a small opening. The dog manipulates the toy to get the treats to fall out. Other such toys are more elaborate, requiring the dog to open small compartments or push a lever to get at the treat. These toys can supply some exercise, both physical and mental. If your dog is anxious when left alone, this type of toy can give him something else to think about other than the fact that he's alone.

No matter what kind of toys you buy for your dog, always supervise play until you know just how he's going to treat that toy and always throw away any toy that is in danger of being broken into small pieces or is worn and dirty.

UN-STUFFED TOYS

If you don't want to deal with stuffing and squeakers, there are dog toys that have no stuffing; they are just a flat length of fake fur. Your dog may still try to rip it apart, but at least you won't have a mess to contend with.

No one tells you when you're considering getting a dog that one of the hardest things you'll ever have to do is open the blister pack that the dog toy comes in. Compared to opening blister packs, housetraining is a breeze, cleaning up after your dog is a snap, and teaching him tricks is a cinch.

Opening a toy's blister pack is an almost impossible task, and there's no easy way to do it. Scissors are an obvious choice, but most of these packs are too thick and tough, and even trying to poke a starter hole with scissors means you run the risk of the scissors slipping and putting that starter hole in your hand. Box cutters generally work, but, again, you risk slicing off a finger or two. I've found that a can opener works very well,

but it leaves razor-sharp edges on the plastic, so you may find yourself once again needing bandages.

While you could just give your dog the entire package (teeth that can crack bone must surely be able to chew through a plastic blister pack!), your dog would run the same risk that you would; shards of plastic could easily cut your dog's lips or gums.

The ideal solution would be for toy manufacturers to create two types of packaging, rather like pill bottles that come in "child-resistant" and "easy-to-open." There may be some people who would opt for the bulletproof version, but I know that I'd reach for the "easy-to-open" version every time.

Throughout this book are suggestions of what you'll need to buy for your dog, and all of these suggestions are valid, but one item that's a must-have is a yardstick. I'm not sure where you get yardsticks anymore. We have four, and we didn't pay for any of them. Two came from lumber yards, and one has the logos of several businesses; it was obviously a giveaway somewhere. The fourth was from Woolworth's. That is an old one, so maybe we did buy that one. The point is that they are useful items to have around if you have a dog.

Sooner or later, your dog will knock a toy or a ball or a bone or a treat under something, and that's when you'll need a yardstick. I guarantee that the toy or treat or whatever will be too far back for you to reach, assuming there's enough clearance for you to get your arm under the couch, chair, etc., in the first place.

Don't think that you can just ignore that item under the couch or stove. The minute it disappears, it will become your dog's favorite thing, and he will *not stop* trying to reach it. He will sniff and

scratch and paw and otherwise make a nuisance of himself until you get the yardstick and rescue the out-of-reach treasure. As a bonus, in addition to retrieving the lost item, the yardstick will bring out any dust bunnies that have grown back there.

Sometimes, dogs knock things into places where even a yardstick will be of no help. If you have floor registers, the grates won't usually accommodate large toys or balls, but small treats are another matter. Many people frown on feeding dogs other than at mealtimes, but, at our house, our dogs share such goodies as popcorn and small cheese crackers. Occasionally, one of these goodies falls down through the register.

If something tasty falls through the grate, it's lost. That doesn't stop our dogs from whining and digging and generally interrupting our television viewing time. That's when I start chewing gum. I rarely chew gum, but I keep a pack for emergencies. Once I've softened up the stick of gum, I push it onto the end of a drinking straw, which I can easily fit through one of the grate openings and use it to retrieve the lost tidbit.

Training
and Activities

You can train your dog using the directions in a good book, but if you can find an available class in your area, it can be a better option. In a class, if there's something you don't understand, you can ask an instructor. Also, signing up for a class commits you to training. Each week, your dog will be expected to know some specific behavior, which means that you will have to set aside time to work with him. Knowing you have that deadline will encourage you to train rather than putting it off. Another benefit of a class is that being with the other dogs and people is a good part of socializing your dog.

Training classes have progressed since I started in dogs more than thirty years ago. Then, it was all about control and using a choke collar. Using treats was frowned upon, especially in obedience. You couldn't use treats in the ring, went the reasoning, so why use them to train? A good trainer made sure that the dog knew what he was supposed to do before being corrected by a jerk on the collar. A bad trainer just jerked the collar.

My first Corgi was always so alert that he never would do an automatic sit during heel training. He'd walk in a heel position, and he'd stop when I stopped, but he didn't

When your dog is a bit older, there are beginning, intermediate, and advanced obedience classes as well as classes designed for specific performance events from rally to agility to tracking and everything in between. There are also trick-training classes if you want to have some fun.

Training, whether formal or informal, is a great way to bond with your dog. So, find a trainer who believes in a kinder, gentler method of training, with or without a clicker (turn the page for more information about clickers), so that you're prepared once you and your new dog are ready to begin training classes.

want to sit when we stopped. I shudder to remember how many times I jerked his neck, to no avail. But he loved food. Today, I'd have trained him using food rewards, and I believe he'd have learned quickly.

Ken McCort, a certified master instructor with Pet Partners' animal-assisted therapy program, says we punish dogs because we can. I've seen Ken work with wolves, teaching them to sit and go to the heel position. He does it with rewards. If he tried harsh methods, he'd be dead.

Formerly, training classes were for dogs six months and older, who'd had all their shots. Today, many new owners like to take advantage of puppy socialization classes when their puppies have had only the first one or two boosters. Puppy classes can help teach your dog to interact with other dogs while building a foundation in the basic commands.

This is not a training book, but clicker training is such an effective and positive way to train a dog that it deserves a mention. Clicker training is not new—it originally was used to train aquatic mammals—but it has gained in popularity over the years. Clicker training enables you to work at a distance from your dog, which is especially helpful when training for performance events.

The clicker is a small handheld plastic box that makes a clicking sound when pressed. You can buy a clicker at a pet-supply store; some clicker-training books come with a clicker. The sound the clicker makes acts as a marker to tell the dog that a particular action is correct. Then, a reward immediately follows. You should offer very small food rewards, no larger than a pea for a big dog and even smaller for small dogs. You can use whatever appeals to your dog, preferably something that he can eat quickly. Bits of cheese and hot dogs are popular, as are bits of liver. You can also cut up pieces of soft commercial dog treats. Just choose something that is easy to handle and not too messy. You don't want to stain your clothing or have to continuously wipe off your hands.

The first step in clicker training is to "charge the clicker," which basically teaches your dog that when he hears the clicker, he's going to get a reward. To charge the clicker, click and treat ten to twelve times in a row. Once your dog understands that the click sound means good things, you can start to train.

There are three ways to use clicker training. The easiest to understand is *luring*. With luring, you use your food reward to guide the dog into whatever behavior you want and then you click and give him the food. For example, by gradually moving the treat back over the dog's head, you can lure him into a sit. Click and treat when he's in position. Eventually, you can name the behavior with the verbal cue "sit," and when your dog hears you say "sit," he will do it without the lure, and you can again click and treat.

The second technique is *shaping*. With shaping, you work on a behavior in increments. For example, an owner wants to teach her dog to go to a specific spot when she needs the dog to be out of the way or when someone comes to the door. She uses

a small mat or rug to mark the spot. She will click and treat the dog for each step that leads to the eventual desired behavior of lying down on the mat. She clicks and treats when the dog walks across the mat. Then, when the dog actually stops on the mat, she will click for that and stop clicking for walking across the mat. When the dog sits on the mat, she starts clicking and treating for that behavior only. Finally, when the dog lies down on the mat, she clicks and treats for that behavior only. She gradually adds the verbal cue "place" or "go to your mat," and the dog will head for his spot and lie down.

Capturing is the third technique, in which you click and treat your dog when you catch him doing something that you want him to do. You may see that your dog likes to curl up for a nap in a particular spot, so you put a rug or blanket there. When your dog curls up in the spot on his own, you click and treat. Or, maybe you think it would be fun to be able to ask your dog if he is sleepy and have

him yawn as a response. Every time your dog yawns, click and treat. Eventually, you can name the behavior ("are you sleepy?"), and your dog will respond on cue.

Clicker training takes patience, but the more you use it, the faster your dog will catch on. Many dogs will begin offering all of the behaviors they know, hoping to get that reward. When that light bulb goes off for your dog, and he understands the game, you can teach him just about anything, and you'll both enjoy the process. It will be a game for you both.

VERBAL CUES
You don't have to use a clicker with your dog; you can choose a word as your marker. The advantage to the clicker is that it is the same sound every time; there's no vocal inflection. If you decide you want to use a word, use the same word, such as "good" or "yes," every time. Don't switch between the two!

Canine Good Citizen (CGC) is an American Kennel Club (AKC) program that evaluates a dog's overall training and behavior. The CGC test is a series of ten exercises conducted by an official AKC CGC examiner. If your dog passes this test, he receives a certificate from the AKC, and you may use the initials CGC after your dog's name. This suffix tells people that your dog has good manners in public.

Essentially, your dog needs to know how to sit, lie down, and stay; he must allow strangers to approach and touch him; and he must not overreact to other dogs. The ten CGC exercises are as follows:

- *Accepting a friendly stranger.* This test assesses the dog's reaction when a stranger approaches the dog and owner. The

CGC EXAMINERS

Many dog trainers are either certified as CGC examiners or will know someone who is. Even if your trainer isn't an examiner, he or she will teach CGC behaviors, which are the behaviors covered in almost all basic obedience classes.

stranger ignores the dog, greets the handler with a few words and a handshake, and then moves on. The dog must not be shy but should also not show any resentment toward the stranger.

- *Sitting politely for petting.* With the dog in a sitting position beside the handler, the tester approaches and pets the dog. The dog may stand and should accept the petting calmly without cringing or trying to get away, and he must not show any aggression.
- *Appearance and grooming.* The owner supplies a comb or brush, and the tester gently brushes the dog, looks at the ears, and picks up each foot to show that the dog will be well behaved at both the groomer's and the veterinarian's.
- *Walking on a loose lead.* The handler walks the dog, stopping now and then. The dog doesn't have to be in a perfect heel position or sit when the handler stops, but the lead should be loose and the dog should stop when the handler stops.
- *Walking through a crowd.* The next test adds at least three people to the walking

THE OWNER'S RESPONSIBILITY

For your dog to take the CGC test, you must sign the AKC's Responsible Dog Owners Pledge. By doing so, you commit to properly caring for your dog and acting courteously with him in public places.

exercise. As the dog and handler move around the people, the dog can be interested but shouldn't jump up or pull.

- *Sit and down on command/staying in place.* The dog must sit and lie down on command. Then, the handler puts the dog in either the sit or down position, tells the dog to stay, walks to the end of the 20-foot line provided by the tester, and then returns to the dog and releases him.
- *Coming when called.* The handler leaves the dog, walks about 10 feet away, and then calls the dog, who should respond by going to the handler.
- *Reaction to another dog.* The handler and dog approach another dog and handler.

The two people chat for a minute and shake hands before moving on. While the dog may be curious, he should not move toward the other dog.

- *Reaction to distraction.* The tester creates distractions, which could include dropping a folding chair, having someone run past the dog, or knocking a cane or crutch onto the floor. The dog may startle a bit or be curious, but he shouldn't overreact by barking or trying to run away.
- *Supervised separation.* The final exercise tests how the dog reacts to being left alone. The handler gives the lead to the tester and then walks out of sight for three minutes. The dog doesn't need to stay in any one position, but he shouldn't whine, bark, or pace.

Once you've passed the CGC test, you may want to go further with obedience training, perhaps even with the goal of competing in obedience or rally. Even if the CGC is the only training you ever do, your dog will have learned the basics for being a "good citizen."

If you love the idea of competing with your dog without too much physical effort, maybe the conformation ring will suit you. Conformation shows are what you most often see on television—for example, the Westminster Kennel Club Dog Show. These shows were developed to show off breeding stock, so each dog is judged by its respective breed standard. The best example of the breed, in the eyes of the judge, will win.

American Kennel Club (AKC) conformation shows are restricted to AKC-registered purebred dogs who are neither spayed nor neutered. To enter a show, fill out an entry form and send it to whatever superintendent is in charge of that particular show. This is much easier

than it used to be because now it's possible to enter online and pay through PayPal. Entries typically close two weeks before the show.

For competition, dogs are divided into classes, including six to nine months old, nine to twelve months old, twelve to eighteen months old, Novice, Bred-by-Exhibitor, American-Bred, and Open. The most entries are usually found in the puppy classes, Bred-by-Exhibitor, and Open.

Males and females (dogs and bitches) are shown in separate classes. The winners of each class then are judged in the "winners" class, with a Winners Dog and a Winners Bitch going on to compete for Best of Breed along with any dogs who have already completed their championships. Only the Winners Dog and Winners Bitch receive any points toward their championships. A dog is awarded a championship after accumulating fifteen points, including two "majors." Winning dogs may earn from one to five points, depending on how many total animals are entered. A "major" is a win of three, four, or five points.

All Best of Breed winners in each breed then move on to the group competition, where they compete with all breed winners in their group (Hound, Sporting, etc.). If the group winner defeats dogs with major points, the winner also acquires those points. The seven group winners then advance to Best in Show competition.

FOR MORE INFO...
Many shows and their locations can be found at InfoDog.com.

UKC SHOWING

United Kennel Club (UKC) conformation shows are a bit different from AKC shows. In UKC shows, no professional handlers are allowed, and there are classes for neutered dogs. An advantage to UKC shows is that there are frequently two shows on the same day, so you could enter and compete in four shows in one weekend instead of just two. Another nice feature is that you can often enter the show the same day, which adds more flexibility to your schedule. Check the UKC's website (www.ukcdogs.com) to find out more.

To earn a Grand Championship, a dog must have his championship and then must earn twenty-five points with at least three majors. From the AKC website: "The majors must be won under three different judges, and at least one other judge must award some of the remaining points—so you need to win under at least four different judges. Also, at least one Champion of Record must be defeated at three of these shows."

Grand Championship points are awarded to finished champions who place as either Winners, Best of Opposite Sex, Select Dog, or Select Bitch. These points are based on the number of entrants of their own sex that they defeated. In addition, if your dog gets this far, the AKC offers four levels of Grand Championship: bronze, silver, gold, and platinum. "The Bronze Grand Championship will require 100 points, the Silver Grand Championship will require 200 points, the Gold Grand Championship will require 400 points, and the Platinum Grand Championship will require 800 Grand Championship points."

All of this can be a bit confusing, but once you've started doing it, it becomes much easier. Also, when you are just starting out, you won't need to keep track of all this information. Just getting to the correct ring for your class is enough to think about!

If you think you'd like to show in conformation, talk to your breeder; she's going to be your best teacher. If your breeder is too far away to easily mentor you, join a local all-breed club. Clubs generally have handling classes to help you prepare your dog for the ring, and if you can find someone else in your breed to give you handling and show grooming advice, that's even better. Maybe you can travel to some shows with a more experienced handler and learn by watching. Conformation showing can be intimidating, but it can also be great fun, and it's a wonderful way to spend time with your dog and with others who are passionate about their dogs.

DID YOU KNOW?

The maximum number of points that any dog can earn at an AKC show is five points in regular competition.

In many cases, people get dogs for companionship, and that's enough for them. They take their dogs for walks, play fetch, and share their couches. A dog may be a pal for the children and may sound the alarm if someone comes to the door. He may know basic commands, such as "sit" and "down." Some people, though, like to do more with their dogs, and that's where performance events come in.

There are performance events to fit just about all dogs and their humans. You can choreograph a dance routine for the two of you to perform together, run through an agility course beside your dog, or watch your dog work at a nosework test or an earthdog trial.

Many performance events, such as herding, lure coursing, hunt tests, and field trials, are designed to show off a dog's natural ability. Different breeds were bred for different tasks, and these events showcase a dog's instinctual reaction to a particular situation. In many cases, dogs need very little training, especially at the beginning levels, for performance events; their instincts tell them what to do, and there's nothing more thrilling than watching dogs do what they were bred to do.

If an organization like the AKC or the UKC is holding these events, you can earn titles that reflect your dog's skills and successes. Generally, these events are group-specific, although there are exceptions. For instance,

AKC herding trials are open to all dogs from the Herding Group as well as certain other breeds, including the Rottweiler and the Samoyed. Other popular events, such as obedience, rally, agility, and dock diving, are open to all purebred and mixed-breed dogs.

Still other events may not be formally recognized by a registry organization but have their own governing bodies through which titles are issued. Treibball, freestyle dance, and skijoring are three such sports.

No matter what kind of dog you have, there is an activity that you can try. Whether you earn an obedience championship or never get out of a basic obedience class, any activity where you and your dog are having fun is worth it.

You can take your dog's natural skills to a competitive level.

75 Agility

Agility is a popular sport in which dogs navigate an obstacle course in the fastest time possible with their handlers running alongside them, directing them through the course. A typical agility course includes jumps, weave poles, tunnels, and seesaws, among other obstacles. With most agility organizations, dogs must be at least fifteen months old to be eligible to compete, and all dogs—including mixed breeds—are welcome, although some breeds do better than others. If you are getting a dog specifically because you want to compete in agility, a Basset Hound, for example, should not be your first choice. However, there are classes designed for dogs of all sizes.

With agility, you're not limited to AKC or UKC events. The North American Dog Agility Council (NADAC), the United States Dog Agility Association (USDAA), and the Dogs on Course in North America (DOCNA) are three agility-focused organizations that offer competition and titles. Although rules and obstacles vary according to the organization, AKC agility, which I will discuss here, gives you the basics of any agility competition.

The obstacles on an agility course are the open tunnel, closed tunnel, pause table, A-frame, seesaw, weave poles, jumps, tire jump, broad jump, and dog walk. The course may include any or all of these obstacles, depending on the class. Dogs may be asked to navigate certain obstacles more than once,

> **DID YOU KNOW?**
> The term "contact obstacles" refers to those obstacles that have a "safety zone," usually painted yellow, at the ends. When going onto and coming off the A-frame, dog walk, and seesaw, the dog must touch that safety zone. This is to help prevent dogs from getting injured by jumping off too soon.

for a total of fourteen to twenty obstacles.

The AKC offers three types of classes. The Standard class includes contact objects. The Jumpers with Weaves class has only jumps, tunnels, and weave poles. The third class, FAST, stands for Fifteen and Send Time. This class tests the handler and dog's accuracy, speed, and distance handling.

Within each class are levels of difficulty, from Novice up to Open, Excellent, and Master. Once a team has earned both an Excellent Standard title and an Excellent

Jumpers title, they may compete for Master Agility Championship title, or MACH.

Classes and levels are further divided by jump heights according to the dogs' sizes. Dogs measuring 11 inches or less at the

VARIATIONS

Agility organizations may have other classes that add more challenge to the sport. The USDAA's Gamblers is such a class. In this class, the handler must stay behind a designated line and direct his or her dog to obstacles in the correct order. The more you progress in the sport, the more you may want to enter trials that offer different challenges.

shoulder jump 8 inches. Dogs above 11 and up to 14 inches jump 12 inches. Dogs measuring more than 14 and up to 18 inches jump 16 inches. Dogs above 16 inches up to 22 inches jump 20 inches. Dogs measuring taller than 22 inches jump 24 inches. There is also a class with 26-inch jumps, entered at the owner's discretion. These height divisions also determine the height of the pause table.

You can buy inexpensive sets of jumps and weave poles for practicing at home, but A-frames and tunnels are generally more expensive. If you want to train for agility, you will probably need to find a training center. With agility's popularity, there's likely to be one in your area.

Barn Hunts

If you think earthdog trials sound like fun, but you don't have a terrier or a Dachshund, then barn hunts could be your sport. The Barn Hunt Association (BHA) offers instinct tests; Novice, Open, Senior, and Master levels; and championships. They also offer fun tests, which give dogs a chance to try the sport. All tests are open to any breed that can fit through "an 18-inch wide by bale-height-tall tunnel," and there are small, medium, and large size divisions as well: 13 inches and under, over 13 to 18 inches, and over 18 inches, respectively. Barn hunt titles are recognized by both the AKC and the UKC. To compete in barn hunts, a dog must have a registration number from the BHA.

In all barn hunt tests, tubes are placed in the tunnels. The tubes may be empty, may contain rat litter, or may contain a rat. There may be turns in the tunnel, ramps, and bridges, with increasing difficulty depending on the level of the test.

At the Novice level (RATN), dogs are given two minutes to find the tube containing the rat. There are three tubes: one empty, one containing litter, and one containing the rat, and at least one of the tubes is elevated. The dog must navigate one tunnel and complete one climb. To earn the title, a dog must qualify at three hunts.

At the Open level (RATO), the dog has two minutes and thirty seconds to find the rats. At this level, there is one empty tube, two tubes with litter, and two tubes with rats. In addition to finding both rats, the dog must navigate an official tunnel and a climb. Three qualifying hunts earn the title.

A dog earns the Senior Barn Hunt (RATS) title with three qualifying hunts. Each hunt lasts three minutes and thirty seconds. At this level, there is one empty tube, three litter tubes, and four rat tubes. The dog must find all four rats, and the tunnel must have two to three turns. The course will also have a climb.

At the Master (RATM) level, things get changed up. The time allotted is four minutes and thirty seconds and there are eight tubes, but the number of rats may be anywhere from one to five and all tubes without a rat will contain rat litter. The number of rats to be found will vary with each competitor.

To win the Barn Hunt Champion (RATCH) title, a dog must qualify ten more times on the Master Hunt course. For Barn Hunt Champion X (RATCHX), dogs must qualify an additional ten times on a Master Hunt course. If you want to keep competing, each additional level will earn you a number after the RATCHX (i.e., RATCHX2, RATCHX3, and so on).

This is a sport where only the dog does the work, so if you have couch-potato tendencies, this might be just the game for you to give your dog some exercise and fun.

Dancing with your dog can be a great outlet, and neither you nor your dog need to wear a ball gown or tuxedo—you just need to learn to move together to whatever music you've chosen. There are two major organizations that offer competitive canine–human dancing: the Canine Freestyle Federation (CFF) and the World Canine Freestyle Organization. (WCFO). In general, the WCFO is less strict, so there's more leeway in costumes and choreography. In CFF competition, the handler may not touch the dog. The CFF also requires specific moves as a part of each routine.

The CFF offers CanineFreestyle DogWork®, which is a "performance activity for dog and human teams" that trains the teams in "movement behaviors technically, creatively, and artistically." CFF offers titles in Levels I through IV as well as a championship level. As competitors progress through the levels, requirements increase in complexity. For example, at Level III, dogs must move forward, backward, and sideways, and Level IV requires distance work. Teams can comprise one human and one dog, one human and two dogs (brace), and teams of multiple dog–human pairs.

For Gaea Mitchel, past president of CFF, it's about teamwork and, within that framework, the dog. Mitchel says, "The dog–human team is free to meet the requirements in the way that best suits them … each team should present the movement that shows the dog to its best advantage. … Music is chosen to suit the tempo of the dog at the trot. Choreography is crafted to present the dog to its best advantage, showcasing the beauty of the dog's natural movement in harmony with the human. The performance … should present natural movement with the music lending cohesion, the dog being the center of attention. As for attire, we dress to complement the dog, and again never to draw the attention to the handler."

The World Canine Freestyle Organization describes the sport as "simply dancing with dogs to music. It is a fun sport for the owners and dogs, and the audience. Based on basic obedience training, it adds other dimensions such as music, timing, costuming, routine development, showmanship."

The WCFO offers bronze, silver, and gold levels of proficiency in both Musical Freestyle and Heelwork to Music. Creativity and innovation are encouraged in Musical Freestyle, with any move allowed as long as neither dog nor handler is in danger. The WCFO's website says, "Distance work, weaves, jumps, send-outs, and/or innovative new moves are encouraged and … may be performed from any position." Certain

> **LEARN MORE**
> For complete rules and regulations for both CFF (www.canine-freestyle.org) and WCFO (www.worldcaninefreestyle.org), visit their websites. These sites will also give you information on where to find competitions so that you can experience them firsthand and talk to participants.

movements are required, depending on the level of competition.

Heelwork to Music routines are more structured, and dog and handler should remain close to each other throughout the routine. There should be no distance work, no jumps of any kind, and no weaving through legs or arms. Heelwork, for the purposes of Heelwork to Music, is not limited to the traditional obedience position but is defined as "any position between the handler and the dog within 360-degree radius and includes, but is not limited to: right heel; left heel; face-to-face; face-to-back; back-to-back; back-to-face; and all angled positions between handler and dog within 360 degrees."

Dock diving is a great way to have fun with your dog, and it's a great way for your dog to expend some energy. Both the AKC and the UKC recognize titles from dock diving organizations; the AKC recognizes titles earned from North American Diving Dogs (NADD), and the UKC works in conjunction with Ultimate Air Dogs. Both of these organizations offer Novice, Junior, Senior, Master, and either Ultimate or Elite levels, as well as championship titles. A third organization, DockDogs, offers categories such as Big Air, Speed Retrieve, and Extreme Vertical.

While all three organizations have slightly different names for their events, there are three basic events in dock-dog competitions. The first is basically a long jump for dogs. While the handler holds the dog, someone throws a toy or bumper into the water. The handler than releases the dog, who runs the length of the dock and jumps out into the water. Distance is measured from the end of the dock to where the tail set of the dog breaks the water's surface. There are size divisions, so I could compete with my Corgi and he would not be judged against a Labrador Retriever.

can jump. A bumper is suspended eight feet out from the dock and the dog must leap and retrieve the toy. The height is raised in 2-inch increments as the competition progresses.

You don't need to have a water-retrieving breed to compete in dock-dog competition; any dog willing to jump into the water can compete. There are many class divisions for different-sized dogs. While many sporting breeds seem to be naturals at this sport, many other types of dog seem to love it just as much as the Labradors do. One warning, though: many dogs with pushed-in or turned-up noses don't do well in water. Bulldogs and Pugs typically sink, and others can get too much water in their noses and drown.

Even if your dog is a fetching fool, don't just assume that he will know what to do in dock diving—you will need to show him. If you have your own pool, you're ahead of the game. If you have steps or a ladder into your pool, show your dog where they are and how to use them; he needs to know how to get out of the pool. Alternatively, put a ramp in the pool. Most dock-diving pools have ramps for dogs to use when exiting. Don't let your dog panic or get tired when swimming.

The second type of event, the retrieve, is when a toy or bumper is suspended just above the water's surface, and the dog needs to leap and grab the toy. The third event, vertical jumping, measures how high your dog

The Dog Scouts of America is a program that allows you and your dog to earn merit badges, similar to the way Boy Scouts and Girl Scouts can earn badges. Categories in which you can earn badges include agility, with nine different badges; community service; nosework; sports, such as treibball, flyball, rally, and pulling; tricks; backpacking; water rescue; and canine massage.

For your dog to become a Dog Scout of America, you have to pass a written test, and

your dog has to pass a test that evaluates his training and behavior. Many of the elements of the dog's test are similar to those of the Canine Good Citizen test, but the Dog Scouts test has a free-heeling component and a "leave it" test with food. You can take the test with a scoutmaster, but if there is no one in your immediate area, you will need to record your test, during a period of three days to six months, to submit to the organization.

There's a handbook on the organization's website (www.dogscouts.org) that lists the steps you and your dog need to follow to become a Dog Scout. It takes work on your part as well as the dog's, but that challenge can strengthen the bond between you.

Earthdog trials are designed to show off the ability of certain terriers, and Dachshunds, to find rats. Since finding vermin was in the terriers' original job description, you don't even need to do much training.

The AKC, Jack Russell Terrier Club of America (JTRCA), and American Working Terrier Association (AWTA) are the largest groups offering this type of terrier trial. All three organizations use caged rats as quarry, and their rules demand humane treatment of the rats. There are smaller groups that actually go out into the field, find a woodchuck den, and have the dogs dig the animal out. If you'd rather not see an animal killed, ask before you enter.

The following breeds are eligible for AKC trials: Australian Terrier, Bedlington Terrier, Border Terrier, Cairn Terrier, Cesky Terrier, Dachshund, Dandie Dinmont Terrier, Glen of Imaal Terrier, Lakeland Terrier, Manchester Terrier, Miniature Bull Terrier, Miniature Pinscher, Miniature Schnauzer, Norfolk Terrier, Norwich Terrier, Parson Russell Terrier, Rat Terrier, Russell Terrier, Scottish Terrier, Sealyham Terrier, Silky Terrier, Skye Terrier, Smooth Fox Terrier, Welsh Terrier, West Highland White Terrier, Wire Fox Terrier, and Yorkshire Terrier. Some of the larger terriers are excluded because of their size, but don't worry; if you have one of those breeds, you can compete in barn dog tests.

Earthdog trials require a dog to navigate a 9 × 9-inch tunnel to reach a caged rat, or rats, at the end of the tunnel. The AKC offers Junior Earthdog (JE), Senior Earthdog (SE), and Master Earthdog (ME) titles. There is also an Intro to Quarry level for beginners, which has a short (10-foot) tunnel with one turn.

Smooth Dachshund puppy

Norwich Terrier

Parson Russell Terrier puppy

In JE, the tunnel is 30 feet long with three 90-degree turns. To earn the title, the dog must qualify at two trials. In SE, the tunnel and turns are the same as in JE, but there's also a false den and exit, and the handler must call the dog out of the tunnel at the end of the trial (the rats are removed first). Three qualifying trials earn the dog the SE title. The ME title is the hardest, with a false entrance, den, and exit. The dog must go to the correct entrance and "honor" another dog, which means that the dog waits while the other dog works. Four qualifying trials are necessary for this title.

The JRTCA offers go-to-ground trials for Jack Russell Terriers. The AWTA holds den trials in which the dogs enter artificial earth dens or burrows instead of the wooden tunnels used by the AKC and the JRTCA; the dens are

Dandie Dinmont Terrier

lined so that there's no danger of the earth collapsing and trapping a dog. The AWTA recognizes the following breeds for den-trial competition: Australian Terrier, Bedlington Terrier, Border Terrier, Cairn Terrier, Cesky Terrier, Dachshund, Dandie Dinmont Terrier, Fell Terrier, Fox Terrier, Glen of Imaal Terrier, Jack Russell Terrier, Jagdterrier, Lakeland Terrier, Norwich Terrier, Norfolk Terrier, Patterdale Terrier, Scottish Terrier, Sealyham Terrier, Skye Terrier, Welsh Terrier, and West Highland White Terrier. The AWTA will also accept mixed-breeds or breeds not specifically mentioned as long as they can easily fit into a 9-inch artificial-earth tunnel.

The AKC suggests encouraging your dog to follow scents before trying earthdog trials. If you see a squirrel or rabbit, take your dog to the spot where you saw the animal and pat the ground, encouraging your dog to sniff. Once he knows that you are helping him find the scent of an animal, he needs to get used to going into an enclosed, dark space. You can even build a tunnel of cardboard boxes and then throw a toy into the tunnel for your dog to retrieve. If you don't want to keep rats yourself, accustom your dog to their scent by asking a pet store to give you some of the dirty bedding when they clean the rat cages. Most terriers are not going to need much encouragement. It's in their genes to go after small furry critters and to follow them into dark, narrow places.

Launched in 2016, the AKC's Fast CAT is open to any breed or mixed-breed older than twelve months. It's a timed 100-yard dash on the level, with no turns. Dogs run singly, chasing a lure, and each dog's timed run is converted into miles per hour, which is then translated into points toward titles.

Scoring is based on a handicap system determined by the height of the dog at the withers. For dogs 18 inches tall or greater, the handicap is 1.0. For dogs 12 inches tall up to just below 18 inches, the handicap is 1.5. For dogs shorter than 12 inches, the handicap is 2.0. As an example of how the handicap is used, a Greyhound might finish the course in less than five seconds, meaning that he was running at 40 miles per hour. The Greyhound would win 40 points, which is the handicap number (1) times the miles per hour (40). An Italian Greyhound, which would have a handicap number of 1.5, could finish the course with a speed of 24 miles per hour, so that dog would get 36 points, which is 1.5 times 24.

DID YOU KNOW?
The conversion chart that is part of the AKC's Fast CAT rules and regulations uses a Greyhound and a Whippet as examples, but don't expect to find your breed anywhere on the chart. The other animals listed are a squirrel, which would finish the course at the equivalent speed of 12 miles per hour, and a chicken at 9 miles per hour.

A dog who earns 150 points is awarded the BCAT title; the DCAT title requires 500 points, and the FCAT title requires 1,000 points. After earning the FCAT, dogs can add numbers to their title (e.g., FCAT2, FCAT3, and so on) for every additional 500 points earned.

If you're looking for a sport that doesn't require much in the way of equipment or training, and your dog will chase a lure for 100 yards, Fast CAT may be just the sport for you.

Greyhounds don't always go fast!

The AKC offers field trials for pointers, retrievers, spaniels, Beagles, Basset Hounds, and Dachshunds to judge the dogs' hunting ability. Dogs who earn the required number of points become Field Champions. Further accumulation of points leads to a Grand Field Championship. In all field trials, competing dogs must be six months of age or older.

Breeds eligible to compete in field trials for pointers include the Brittany, English Setter, German Shorthaired Pointer, German Wirehaired Pointer, Gordon Setter, Irish Red and White Setter, Irish Setter, Pointer, Spinone Italiano, Vizsla, Weimaraner, Wirehaired Pointing Griffon, and Wirehaired Vizsla.

AKC field trials for retrievers are open to the Chesapeake Bay Retriever, Curly-Coated Retriever, Flat-Coated Retriever, Golden Retriever, Irish Water Spaniel, Labrador Retriever, and Nova Scotia Duck Tolling Retriever. Since the purpose of retrievers, according to the AKC, is "to seek and retrieve fallen game when ordered to do so," retriever

Basset Hound

field trials are designed to best demonstrate that skill. The dogs are also "expected to retrieve any type of game bird under all conditions." It's important that the retriever waits until he is sent to retrieve by his handler, and the dog should also be able to "mark," or

FIELD-TRIAL BASICS

While there are differences depending on the level of training a dog has achieved, this quote from the AKC is for Gun Dog Stakes but sums up what all of the trials are about. The dog "must cover adequate ground but never range out of sight for a length of time that would detract from its usefulness as a practical hunting dog. The dog must locate game, must point staunchly, and must be steady to wing and shot. Intelligent use of the wind and terrain in locating game, accurate nose, and style and intensity on point, are essential."

notice and remember, where a bird has fallen. When sent by his handler, the dog should be able to go directly to where the bird is.

AKC field trials for spaniel breeds reward the hunting abilities of the Cocker Spaniel, English Cocker Spaniel, and English Springer Spaniel. Trials simulate a day in the field, and dogs are judged on "their game-finding, ability, steadiness, and retrieving. In game-finding, the dog should cover all his ground on the beat, leaving no game in his territory and showing courage in facing cover. Dogs must be steady to wing and shot and obey all commands. When ordered to retrieve, they should do this tenderly and with speed." There may also be a water test that requires the dog to retrieve from water.

Other spaniel breeds have hunting styles different from the aforementioned spaniels, and their registration numbers are too low to warrant several additional types of trials. These other breeds may participate in *hunt tests*, which are judged on a pass/fail basis rather than a points-based competition.

AKC field trials for Beagles, Bassets, and Dachshunds are similar in that all three of these breeds are tested on their skill and ability to follow the trail of rabbits. Classes offered at trials are brace (two dogs running), small pack (seven dogs), large pack (twenty-five dogs), and gundog brace, where a gun is fired to test for gun shyness. No matter the breed or the number of dogs running, the rules say that "credit is earned for searching ability, pursuing ability, accuracy in trailing, proper use of voice, endurance, adaptability, patience, determination, proper degree of independence, cooperation, controlled competitive spirit, intelligence displayed when searching or in solving problems encountered along the trail, and success in accounting for game."

DID YOU KNOW?
The Amateur Field Trial Clubs of America (AFTCA) also offers field trials.

German Shorthaired Pointer puppy

83

Flyball is a team sport made for fast dogs who love to retrieve. In this sport, teams of four dogs run a relay race: they jump over four hurdles, press a pedal that releases a tennis ball, catch the ball, and return back to the starting point over the four jumps. The team with the fastest time wins. The specifications discussed here are those of the North American Flyball Association.

The starting line is 6 feet from the first jump, with 10 feet between each jump and 15 feet between the last jump and the flyball box that releases the ball. The jump height is determined by the height of the smallest dog on the team. The jump is set at 5 inches below the height at the withers of the smallest dog, with jumps no less than 7 inches high and no greater than 14 inches high. You might want a short dog on your team to lower the height of the jumps, but you need to consider whether you are then losing the speed with which a taller dog might complete the course.

Border Collies are top performers in flyball.

Teams may be made up of four dogs of the same breed or of four dogs of different breeds or mixes, and the two types of teams compete in their own groups. Same-breed teams are called Performance teams, and they earn Flyball titles; mixed teams are called Multibreed teams, and they earn Multibreed titles. Titles are Flyball/Multibreed Dog, Excellent, Champion, Champion Silver, Champion Gold, Master, Master Excellent, Master Champion, ONYX, and Grand Champion.

The AKC currently recognizes three titles: Flyball Dog Champion, which requires 500 points; Flyball Dog Master, which requires 5,000 points; and ONYX, which requires 20,000 points.

HOW IT'S SCORED

Points are awarded toward titles based on the speed of the runs. If a team finishes in less than 24 seconds, each dog on the team receives 25 points toward a title; less than 28 seconds but more than 24, and then 5 points; and less than 32 seconds but more than 28, each dog receives one point.

MORE INFO

Everything you ever wanted to know about flyball is at www.flyball.org, the home page of the North American Flyball Association (NAFA). There's also information at www.flyballdogs.com.

I love herding. I have tried the sport only on a very small scale with a couple of my Corgis, but I find it also very fun to watch. I am always amazed at the way instinct kicks in and dogs who have never seen sheep before know what they are supposed to do. There are several organizations that offer herding trials, and most allow any of the herding breeds to compete. The AKC allows some other breeds as well.

The United States Border Collie Handlers' Association (USBCHA) trials follow the pattern set by Great Britain's International Sheep Dog Society, the original registry for Border Collies. There are classes for different levels of training, including Novice, Nursery, and Open. In Novice classes, the handler may accompany the stock throughout the course, while at the higher levels, the handler remains in a fixed position until moving to the pen to assist the dog in penning. The higher levels also include "shedding," or separating designated sheep from the group.

There are trials for cattle as well as for sheep. Titles are not given in connection with USBCHA trials. In an open trial, handler and dog start with 100 points. The judge takes off points for errors as the dog works, and the team has ten minutes to complete the course. First, there's the *outrun* (20 points), in which the dog runs in a large semicircle that puts him behind the sheep. Then comes the *lift* (10 points), where the dog gets into position

> ### DID YOU KNOW?
> In all trials or tests held by all organizations, "gripping" is strictly forbidden. Gripping is when a dog grabs a sheep with his mouth.

to start moving the sheep. In the *fetch* (20 points), the dog moves the sheep toward the handler and through a gap in two panels. The dog continues to move the sheep up to and around the handler. Next is the *drive* (30 points). The dog moves the sheep off to the right, through a gap in another set of panels, then back across the field (the *cross drive*) and through another set of panels on the left, and then back to the handler.

Then there's the *shed* (10 points). One of the sheep wears a red collar, and the dog and handler have to separate that sheep, plus one other, and hold them away from the other

Cardigan Welsh Corgi

sheep until the judge calls the shed. Then, the sheep rejoins its buddies, and it is time for the dog to put them all into a small pen (10 points).

Many breeders of herding breeds have their dogs tested for herding instinct through the AKC, and dogs of many different breeds have won Herding Champion titles. The American Herding Breeds Association (AHBA) reports that competition at the most advanced levels is dominated by Border Collies, Australian Shepherds, and Shetland Sheepdogs, but that many other breeds hold AHBA herding championships, including German Shepherd Dogs, Cardigan and Pembroke Welsh Corgis, Rottweilers, Doberman Pinschers, Poodles, and Schnauzers.

Samoyed puppy

While many serious herding trialers have their own sheep, you can live sheep-free and still enjoy the fun of working with your dog and watching his instincts develop. You'll need some kind of livestock for practice, but many areas have local herding clubs with access to stock, which may be a flock of ducks instead of sheep. The ideal is to find an experienced competitor who's willing to be your mentor.

The world of herding tests and trials is a confusing alphabet soup of initials, especially if you're considering competing in the trials of more than one organization. Just remember that there is a progression from "new at this" to "my dog can do it all." If you're a beginner, start with the simplest level and work your way up. Also, not all courses are like the one previously described, which is a USBCHA Open Class trial. Depending on the organization and the level of expertise of you and your dog, there may be chutes, bridges, gates, and/or water, as well as motorized vehicles, on the course.

American Kennel Club trials are for AKC-registered dogs from the Herding Group and some additional breeds, such as Rottweilers, Samoyeds, Standard and Giant Schnauzers, and Greater Swiss Mountain Dogs. The trials range in difficulty from Started to Intermediate to Advanced. There are also herding instinct tests to test a dog's desire to herd. A dog and handler can work up to the Herding Excellent (HX) title, and, once

a dog has acquired an HX, he can go on to accumulate championship points toward a herding championship (HC).

Stock used in a trial can vary—ducks, geese, turkeys, sheep, goats, or cattle. In addition to a system of points, there is also a time limit of ten minutes at all three AKC levels. All the events are held within an arena or fenced area that varies by size depending on the stock being used.

Australian Shepherd Trial Association (ASTA) courses vary according to what best suits a particular location, type of livestock, and personal preferences. Trials use either point/time or time-only scoring rather than a judged system, and they use sheep and cattle as stock. Awards and placements are given, but there are no titles. While focused on Australian Shepherds, ASTA competitions welcome other breeds.

The Australian Shepherd Club of America (ASCA) Stockdog Program offers three levels of arena trials as well as an open field

"post-advanced" course and a ranch course. The titles Started Trial Dog (STD), Open Trial Dog (OTD), and Advanced Trial Dog (ATD) can be earned on sheep, cattle, and ducks, with lowercase initials after the title indicating the type of stock. The Working Trial Championship (WTCh.) is earned when the dog has earned the advanced title on all three types of stock. The ASCA is a registry for the Australian Shepherd, but its trials are open to all approved herding breeds.

The American Herding Breed Association (AHBA) is open to all herding breeds and herding-breed mixes and offers four types of trial classes, each with three levels, as well as a test program. The Herding Trial Dog program offers HTD I, II, and III levels, and the Herding Ranch Dog program offers HRD I, II, and III levels. Additional titles are offered through the Ranch Large Flock and Herding Trial Arena Dog programs. A herding trial championship is earned by obtaining additional qualifying scores after any Level III title is earned.

I f you have a pointing breed, a retriever, or a spaniel—or, in some cases, an Airedale Terrier, Beagle, Coonhound, Cur, or Feist—you may want to try a hunt test. Hunt tests are not competitive. The dogs compete against only themselves, and they either pass or fail on their own merit; there's no comparison with any other dog. The AKC holds hunt tests for pointing, retrieving, and spaniel breeds as well as the Airedale Terrier. The United Kennel Club UKC offers hunting tests for retrievers, pointers, Beagles, Coonhounds, Curs, and Feists. Further testing options are offered by the North American Hunting Dog Association and the Hunting Retriever Club.

DID YOU KNOW?

In AKC tests, for testing purposes, Irish Water Spaniels are tested as retrievers and Airedale Terriers are tested as spaniels based on their hunting talents.

The format of the AKC tests depends on how the dog hunts and what his breed was developed for, such as finding upland fowl (quail, partridge, grouse, chukar, and pheasant) or leaping into the water after a duck. Of course, some dogs can do both, and even a dog not bred for water retrieving may sometimes be required to retrieve a fallen bird from a body of water.

There are three levels—Junior, Senior, and Master—and more is asked of the dog at each level. To earn the title Junior Hunter (JH), a dog must receive a qualifying score at four different tests. To earn the title Senior Hunter (SH), a dog must either receive a qualifying score at six different tests or already hold the JH title and pass five different tests. The same is true for Master Hunter (MH).

For pointers at the Junior level, judges look for dogs who show a desire to hunt, an ability to find birds, the ability to point, "trainability" (the dog's willingness to respond to his handler's commands), and his response to gunfire (blanks are fired in junior tests).

For the Senior hunt test, the dogs must display all of the junior requirements plus

Airedale Terrier

remain in position after finding a bird until either the bird is shot or the handler releases him. The dog then retrieves the bird. The bracemate must honor the point.

In the Master-level test, more is expected of the dog in terms of response to his handler and honoring his bracemate. The handler may caution a dog honoring a point, but may not restrain the dog nor command the dog to honor.

Retrievers are tested both on land and in water. They, too, must respond well to their handlers and should perform eagerly. On retrieves, a dog is expected to go as directly as possible to the bird and retrieve it promptly to the handler. A dog must also persevere, meaning that he must make every effort to reach the bird, even in dense brush.

Junior dogs are tested on four marks—two on land and two on water—and the dog must bring the bird back to the handler's hand. Senior dogs must complete one land blind, one water blind, one double land mark, and one double water mark. A "double mark" means that there are two birds shot, and the dog must pay attention to, or mark, where both birds fell and retrieve them in the order in which they fell. A "blind" means that the dog can't see where the bird lands. Master dogs must show proficiency in a minimum of five hunting situations, including at least three land and water marks.

Spaniels have their own set of tests, and, in addition, an American Water Spaniel must

receive two passing scores from American Water Spaniel Club water certification events before he can qualify for an AKC hunt test title. As with the pointing and retrieving tests, the dogs are expected to show enthusiasm and to respond well to their handlers.

For a spaniel Junior hunt test, the dog must retrieve two birds on land and one on water. Seniors need to meet this same criteria, with a willingness to work away from the handler and to enter dense cover. A Senior dog must

find, flush, and retrieve two birds on land and one from water as well as a dead bird that neither he nor the handler can see when sent in the bird's general vicinity.

For the Master hunt test, the dog must pass all elements of the Senior test but must also give a "polished and finished" performance. The dog should hunt with a minimum of commands from the handler and should be enthusiastic and independent while at the same time staying within normal shotgun range of the handler (approximately 30–40 yards).

These are bare-bones descriptions of the tests. If you are serious about hunting with your pointer, retriever, or spaniel, explore the rules and regulations. Also remember that requirements, although similar, will be different according to which organization is sponsoring the test.

DID YOU KNOW?

For hunt tests, all dogs are sent into the field in pairs, or braces. In certain exercises, a dog must honor his bracemate by staying and waiting for the other dog to finish a given task.

Sighthounds were bred to pursue game by sight and are generally fast, agile dogs. The sport of lure coursing simulates that pursuit and tests both the dog's agility and his ability to follow prey (in this case, a lure made of white plastic strips). The lure is tied to a cord that runs through a series of pulleys and is laid out in a circular course of between 600 and 1000 yards. The course features four turns that test the dog's agility and ability to follow the "prey." Ideally, the lure stays between 10 and 30 yards in front of the dogs. Dogs must be at least twelve months old to compete.

The AKC offers a pass/fail lure coursing test that is used to test a sighthound's instincts. The club also offers tests for Junior Courser, Senior Courser, and Master Courser titles. In the Junior Courser test, dogs run solo. To earn the Senior Courser title, the dog must have the Junior Courser title and must run with at least one other dog in an Open Stake and earn a qualifying score at four tests under at least two different judges. To earn the Master Courser title, a dog must have the Senior Courser title and must earn 25 scores in Open, Open Veteran, or Specials Stakes.

Lure coursing trials are competitive events in which competing dogs may earn championship points. In an AKC trial, dogs are judged on overall ability (ten points), follow (ten points), speed (ten points), agility (ten points), and endurance (ten points). A dog must earn a score of at least 50 percent of the points to qualify for field championship points. A dog earns a Field Champion title by

Borzoi

acquiring fifteen AKC lure coursing points, which must include at least two majors. The dog can then continue to compete to earn a Lure Courser Excellent title and the additional levels beyond: Lure Courser Excellent II, III, IV, and so on. The Lure Courser Excellent title requires forty-five championship points. The maximum number of points that can be earned in a day is five, and point distribution is based on the dog's breed and number of dogs competing.

The UKC also offers lure coursing tests and trials. Their Coursing Aptitude Test is open to all breeds and all mixed-breed dogs with a UKC performance listing number. The UKC offers three Coursing Aptitude titles: Coursing Aptitude, in which the dog runs alone and must receive three qualifying scores at three different meets; Coursing Aptitude Excellent, in which the dog runs alone, must have the Coursing Aptitude title, and must earn twelve qualifying scores; and Coursing Aptitude Supreme, in which a dog needs the two previous titles, plus fifteen qualifying scores. Coursing Tested titles follow similar progressions, with Coursing Tested, Coursing Tested Excellent, and Coursing Tested Supreme titles available. Levels of championships in lure coursing are Lure Coursing Champion, Grand Lure Coursing

Champion, and Supreme Lure Coursing Champion. With each level, the number of championship points needed increases.

The American Sighthound Field Organization (ASFA) was founded in 1972 to promote the sport of lure coursing. They offer Coursing Proficiency and Coursing Proficiency Excellent titles as well as Field Champion and Veteran Field Champion. Dogs who continue to compete can earn the title Lure Courser of Merit (LCM) title, which is followed by LCM II, LCM III, and so on. ASFA judges award points based on speed (twenty-five), agility (twenty-five), endurance (twenty), enthusiasm (fifteen), and follow (fifteen), for a total of one hundred points.

Rhodesian Ridgeback

osework, like tracking, can be one of the most difficult pursuits for the human half of the team because there's no way to guide the dog. The handler must trust the dog to locate a particular odor or odors and then indicate that find. Writer and nosework enthusiast Kim Campbell Thornton says, "At every class and every trial, I get better at reading her signals, and she gets better at delivering them. Most of all, I've taken to heart the nosework motto: trust your dog."

The National Association of Canine Scent Work (NACSW) and the United Kennel Club (UKC) are the two governing bodies for the sport in the United States. In Canada, it's the Sport Detection Dog Association (SDDA). All three organizations use specific scents that the dogs must find, according to the level of work, and all three offer titles based on the difficulty of the tests.

Nosework dogs are expected to find and indicate scents in four different situations—exterior, interior, vehicle, and container—and to do so in an allotted time, generally up to three minutes. Exterior searches can be complicated by other smells, including other animals, and weather may also play a factor. Interior searches may be limited to one room or, at more advanced levels, may be in more than one room. There can even be a room that has no scent in it at all. Vehicle searches can be any type of vehicle, and there are usually three or more. The scent is always on the outside of the vehicle. Container searches increase in complexity. Beginning levels use plain boxes. At advanced levels, the containers may be luggage, plastic bins, or just about anything. At the lowest level, there is just one odor in each setting. At higher levels, there may be three or more different scents. The NACSW uses birch, anise, and clove. The UKC uses these three plus myrrh and vetiver.

While NACSW offers training classes with certified instructors, if you live in an area that doesn't have any official classes or trials, you can still try nosework as just something fun to do with your dog. An article by Kim Campbell Thornton on Vetstreet.com, titled *Canine Nose Work: A Sport for Dogs Who Love to Sniff*, describes a way to train your dog, starting with your dog finding and eating treats out of open boxes. When your dog finds the box with the treats, he not only gets to eat those treats, but he gets more treats for finding the correct box. Eventually, you add odors, so that the dog starts searching for the scent and being rewarded for the find. It's all positive reinforcement, and that makes it fun for both you and your dog.

The time you put into training will pay off if you enter competitive pursuits.

In regular obedience competition, you must follow the directions of the judge in completing a series of exercises, and you are not allowed to talk to your dog beyond giving the necessary commands. Many people and dogs love obedience for its precision and for the tight bond between handler and dog as they perform each exercise. The following describes AKC competition and will give you an idea of the obedience trials held by other organizations, such as the UKC.

The first level of competition is Novice, for the Companion Dog (CD) title. To earn the title, you must earn 170 points or more out of 200, under three different judges. Furthermore, each exercise has an assigned number of points, and you and your dog must earn at least 50 percent of the points for each exercise.

The heel on lead and figure-eight exercise is worth forty points. In this exercise, the judge will move you around the ring, asking for left and right turns, an about turn, slow and fast paces, and halts. Your dog must remain in the correct heel position during all of this. For the figure-eight, you walk around two ring stewards in a figure-eight pattern, and the judge will call one halt.

The stand for examination is worth thirty points. In this exercise, you will stand your dog, remove the lead, command your dog to stay, and walk about 6 feet away. The judge will approach your dog, touch him lightly, and then step back and tell you to return to your dog, all while your dog remains standing in one spot.

The heel off lead exercise is worth forty points and is identical to the heel on lead except that your dog is off lead. The recall is worth thirty points. In this exercise, you put your dog in a sit-stay, walk across the ring, and, at the judge's signal, call your dog. Your dog must return to you and sit directly in front of you. At another signal from the judge, you give the command to return to the heel position.

The long sit and the long down are worth thirty points each, and all dogs in the class perform these two exercises at the same time. The long sit is for one minute; the long down is for three minutes. In each of these, your dog is in a line with all the other dogs in the class. You give the command to either

> **UKC TITLES**
> The UKC offers three levels of obedience competition with three corresponding titles—United Companion Dog (UCD), United Companion Dog Excellent (UCDX), and United Utility Dog (UUD)—as well as an obedience championship.

"sit-stay" or "down-stay" and walk to the far side of the ring. At the end of the time limit, you return to your dog's right side. Your dog should remain in either the sit or the down position until the judge says "exercise finished."

Open is the next level, and the title at stake is Companion Dog Excellent (CDX). Many of the exercises are similar to those for the CD, but all are done off lead. During the recall, as your dog comes toward you, he must drop into a "down" at your hand signal. You then call him again, and the exercise runs the same as at the CD level. The long sit is for three minutes and the long down for five; this time, you leave the ring and are out of the dog's sight for both exercises. Additional CDX exercises are retrieving and jumping. Your dog will be asked to retrieve a dumbbell on the flat (worth twenty points) and over a high jump (worth thirty points) as well as complete a broad jump.

The next level is Utility, for the Utility Dog (UD) title; at this level, things change radically. There are no group exercises and no individual heeling exercises. Heeling is incorporated into the signal exercise, worth forty points, in which you command your dog solely with hand signals. No verbal commands are allowed. In this exercise, as you are heeling, the judge will command you to stand your dog, leave your dog, down your dog, have your dog sit from the down position, and, finally, execute a recall and a finish (return to heel position). In scent-discrimination exercises, your dog must detect your scent on a set of leather articles and then on a set of metal articles. Each section is worth thirty points.

The directed retrieve is worth thirty points. In this exercise, while you and your dog have your backs turned, the steward drops three white gloves in a row. When you turn to face the gloves, the judge will indicate which glove to retrieve, and you send your dog to the correct glove.

The moving stand and examination is worth 30 points. In this exercise, you heel your dog until the judge tells you to "stand your dog." Without stopping, you tell your dog to stand while you continue moving forward another 10–12 feet. You then turn and face your dog. The judge will examine your dog, just as it's done for the CD, but, this time, instead of returning to your dog, you call your dog to heel.

The final exercise is directed jumping, worth forty points. In this exercise, there are two jumps: a high jump and a bar jump. In this exercise, you send your dog away from you and then give the command to sit. The judge then indicates which of the two jumps your dog is to jump, at which point you signal your dog to jump over the appropriate jump. This is repeated for the second jump.

To earn a Utility Dog Excellent (UDX), your dog must receive a qualifying score in both Open B and Utility B classes ten times. If you still want more, you can work on your dog's Obedience Trial Championship (OTCH).

89 Rally

DID YOU KNOW? At all levels of AKC rally, a qualifying score is 70 or more points out of a possible 100.

Both the AKC and the UKC offer rally and, although there are some differences, if you can compete in one, you shouldn't have any trouble competing in the other. Rally is less formal than obedience. For instance, in obedience competition, you are allowed to give your dog one command only for a specific exercise. Any additional commands will cost you point deductions. In rally, you may give multiple commands, and, although you may not touch your dog, you may encourage him with motions such as slapping your leg. In obedience, a judge issues commands as to what you should do (heel, about turn, halt), but in rally, you follow small signs around the course and perform whatever the signs say. For example, in AKC rally, the judge tells the handler to begin, and the dog and handler proceed at their own pace through the course, on which each station (10 to 20, depending on the level) is designated by a sign. Each of these signs provides instructions regarding the skill that is to be performed.

There are three levels in AKC Rally. At the Novice level, all exercises are performed with the dog on lead. There are ten to fifteen stations at this level.

At the Advanced level, all exercises are performed off lead, and there are twelve to seventeen stations. One of the exercises at this level is a jump. At the Excellent level, there are fifteen to twenty stations, with all exercises performed off lead. Handlers at this level may still encourage their dogs verbally but may not clap or slap their legs. One of the most difficult exercises at this level is the handler backing up three steps while the dog stays in heel position, moving with the handler.

UKC rally also has three levels: United Rally 1, United Rally 2, and United Rally 3. In Rally 1, the handler works the dog on lead. At the higher levels, the dog works off lead. There are fifteen to seventeen stations per course, and handler and dog move at their own pace from start to finish, fulfilling the command on the sign at each station. Rally is a great way to try obedience-type exercises with less pressure because you can encourage your dog and praise him as you advance around the course. After trying rally, you may want to work on further skills and enter the formal obedience ring.

If your dog loves people and has a stable temperament, you might want to consider doing therapy work with him. A therapy dog is not a service dog. A therapy dog can help hospital patients, nursing-home residents, and students. A dog can help with physical therapy by allowing the patient to walk him on a leash or groom him. Many schools have reading programs where students read to therapy dogs. Therapy dogs are also used at disaster sites. Handlers with therapy dogs were some of the first to be allowed into Newtown, Connecticut, following the tragic school shooting in 2012. Therapy dogs also provide support to firefighters and other first responders, helping them cope with tragedy.

While some institutions may allow you to visit with your dog with no certification, many will want to know that your dog meets certain standards and that you have insurance should something happen on their property.

Therapy Dogs International (TDI) and Pet Partners (formerly the Delta Society) are two active nationwide organizations that certify therapy dogs. To become certified, your dog

Therapy dogs can bring smiles to hospital patients of all ages.

must pass a test similar to the CGC test, and you will receive a special ID card upon his passing. With both of these organizations, there is insurance coverage.

With TDI, dogs must be tested by a TDI-certified evaluator. If there isn't an evaluator within a four-hour drive of where you live, you can still apply for limited registration, but you will need proof of graduation from both basic and intermediate obedience, a letter of recommendation from your veterinarian, and letters from institutions you are planning to visit saying that they would welcome visits. There are also health requirements for all TDI-registered dogs.

The Pet Partners program certifies teams for animal-assisted activities, such as nursing-home visits and school reading programs, as well as animal-assisted therapy. With animal-assisted therapy, the handler–dog team works with a professional healthcare provider, such as a physical therapist, to help a patient.

DID YOU KNOW?

The AKC does not certify teams for therapy-dog work, but it does recognize "the great work our dogs are doing" by awarding a Therapy Dog title based on the number of visits made by certified dog–handler teams.

91 Tracking

DID YOU KNOW?
Aging is the time between when a track is laid and when the dog gets to follow it.

Tracking is a sport that you can do with any dog, and all you need for equipment is a harness and a long line of between 20 and 40 feet in length. While training, it will be helpful to have small flags to indicate the trail, and you'll also need scent articles–one cloth, one leather, one plastic, and one metal–with each article being between 2 x 4 inches and 5 x 5 inches. That's it. The dog does the rest.

The AKC offers three tracking titles. TD, or Tracking Dog, is relatively straightforward, with three to five turns in a track, no major obstacles, and two scent articles, one at the beginning and one at the end. The track must be between 440 and 500 yards long and is aged between thirty minutes and two hours. The TDX, or Tracking Dog Excellent, is more difficult, with a longer track of between 800 and 1,000 yards; from five to seven turns; a track that is aged three to five hours; four scent articles, which the dog must indicate he has found; and at least two obstacles, such as a fallen tree, a stream, or a fence. TDX tracks also have two cross-tracks; the dog has to stick to the original track and not follow one of the cross-tracks.

Then there's Variable Surface Tracking. To earn the VST title, dog and handler must first have earned either a TD or a TDX. The length of a VST track is between 600 and 800 yards.

TRACKING TRAITS

Dogs with long ears that drag the ground have an advantage in tracking because those ears help to channel the scent toward their noses. Dogs who drool may also have an advantage because the constant moisture on their lips and ear tips helps encourage the bacterial action on the rafts, thus releasing scent.

THE POWERFUL CANINE NOSE

Dogs' noses are built to gather and identify different scents. For starters, dogs don't get "scent fatigue." A scent is just as strong for a dog an hour later as it was when he first smelled it. The human nose tends to get "tired." A scent we find strong and noticeable at first tends to be less evident the more we smell it.

Then there are the cilia, the tiny hairlike extensions in the lining of the nose that gather the scent. There are 6 to 8 cilia per inch in humans, and 100 to 150 per inch in dogs. The more air breathed in, the more scent gathered. Humans take in about 1.6 cubic inches of air in a breath; dogs take in 6 cubic inches or more.

Dogs also beat humans in the count of scent receptors per square inch in the nose. There are 5 to 20 million scent receptors per square inch in humans and 220 million per square inch, on average, in dogs. Pugs and other short-nosed breeds have fewer receptors. German Shepherd Dogs come close to the 220 million figure. Bloodhounds have about 300 million scent receptors per square inch.

There are no fallen trees to scramble over, but a VST track has between four and eight such obstacles. Both the TDX and the VST track are aged between three and five hours, but a VST track must cross at least three different surfaces, including "vegetation, concrete, asphalt, gravel, sand, hard pan, or mulch." During the three to five hours of aging time, it is likely that dozens of cars, bicycles, and pedestrians will have gone over the track. Also, although wind can blow the scent from the track at any level, VST competitors usually have to contend with the wind currents caused by buildings, which can cause a dog to drift off track.

During the VST test, the dog must find the aforementioned four articles (cloth, leather, plastic, and metal) and indicate each of these articles as he finds them. Generally, handlers train their dogs to sit or down when they find the article because this clearly tells the judge that the dog has found the article.

What exactly is the dog following as he seems to pursue a trail that is invisible to humans? He's following "scent rafts" that have drifted down from the tracklayer. Dying cells are shed from a human at an average of about 40,000 cells per minute. What a dog smells is the gas given off as bacteria work to decompose these cells, thus creating a scent trail. The rafts are carried down and out by the layer of air that surrounds every human.

The speed at which the bacteria will act on the cells is affected by temperature, humidity, and wind. It is harder for a dog to follow a trail on a hot, dry, windy day than on a cooler day with a light rain falling. Moisture is needed for the bacterial action.

DID YOU KNOW?

Dogs who earn all three tracking titles are designated CT, or Champion Tracker.

Treibball (pronounced *try-ball*) began in Germany as a sport for herding dogs who had no animals to herd, but it quickly became popular as a sport for all breeds. The American Treibball Association organizes competitions and has member trainers in various areas of the country who can help you learn the sport. There are also books available on how to teach your dog the skills he needs for treibball.

Treibball is played on a field 100 to 164 feet long and 50 to 82 feet wide, and the ball must stay within the field's boundaries. The goal is a soccer goal or a similar pen, 8 feet high by 24 feet wide. The handler must stay within an 18-foot radius from the center of the goal. Once the ball is in that area, the handler can use a cane or crook to help guide the ball into the goal.

To start, eight large balls are placed in a triangle (think billiard balls) with four in the first row, three in the second, and one in the third. The balls used are ordinary exercise balls or balance balls, either the 45-cm or 75-cm size (about 18 inches or 29½ inches). The dog and handler have fifteen minutes to drive all of the balls into the goal. The dog must do an outrun and then stop and pause to wait for the handler's command before beginning to move the balls. The dog must move the balls with his nose, and, just as in sheep herding, biting is forbidden.

The basic skills your dog will need to know to play treibball are sit, down, and touch

The Collie is a herding breed with a natural talent for treibball.

A long-distance skijoring event is called a *loppet*.

(touching an object with his nose on command), as well as how to turn left and turn right on command. Some people use herding commands, but whatever works best for you is fine. Your dog should also be reliable off lead. With the help of a trainer or a good book on treibball, you and your dog can enjoy herding without the expense and upkeep of a flock of sheep.

Skijoring originated in Norway and is a combination of cross-country skiing and sled-dog racing, with one to three dogs pulling the skier. Any dog who weighs 30 pounds or more and enjoys running in the snow can participate. Many people enjoy skijoring as a great way to get exercise and be outside with their dog or dogs, but there is also competitive racing. The Midwest Skijorers Club (not to be confused with the North American Ski Joring Association, which uses horses instead of dogs) is an organization that hosts competitive racing; it follows the rules of the International Federation of Sleddog Sports (IFSS) and the International Sled Dog Racing Association (ISDRA).

If you just want to enjoy skijoring on your own, you'll need skis, a dog or dogs, a pulling harness for each dog, a hip belt, and a towline to attach the dog's harness to your hip belt. Wait until your dog is an adult before you train him to pull you as you ski.

If you think you'd like to skijor competitively, there are some basics that you and your dog should know before you enter a race. First, since other people will be handling your dog during a race, he needs to be well socialized. Next, your dog should also be good around other dogs. You and your dog also need to know how to pass another team and how to be passed, and you need to practice these maneuvers before you ever enter a race. Another good rule, whether in a race or just out with friends, is to keep a minimum of 20 feet between you and another skijorer.

Weight Pulling & Carting

If you are getting an American Staffordshire Terrier, American Pit Bull Terrier, or a pit bull mix, UKC weight pulling may be just the sport for you. These dogs' strength and willingness to please make them naturals at weight pulling. Northern breeds, such as the Alaskan Malamute, which was bred to pull large loads, will also enjoy pulling, as will breeds like St. Bernards and Rottweilers, which count cart pulling among their original functions, but really any breed can compete in weight pulling with proper training. A

TRAIN WITH CAUTION
Weight pulling can be a great activity for you and your dog, but remember to start slowly with training, building up your dog's strength and stamina to avoid injuries and strains.

American Staffordshire Terriers and related breeds are naturally built for weight pulling.

woman I know has a Miniature Poodle who has successfully competed in weight pulling.

In weight pulling competition, a dog is scored by how much weight he can pull and by the proportion of his body weight to the amount of weight pulled; in this way, a Miniature Poodle is not expected to pull the same weight as a Rottweiler. The dog is attached by a harness to a weighted vehicle that may have wheels or runners or may run on rails or even in snow. Each time, a dog must pull the vehicle 16 feet within one minute. With a wheeled vehicle, the starting load is eight times the dog's body weight. On rails, the weight is ten times the dog's body weight. On snow, the weight is three times the dog's weight. To earn a title, a dog must qualify under three different judges, and there are eight titles available in UKC weight pulling.

There are other opportunities for weight pulling besides UKC events. Lug-Nuts is a program that organizes informal weight pulling events in cities across the country. Some breed clubs, like the Alaskan Malamute Club of America, also

A Bull Terrier gets ready to pull.

offer weight-pulling opportunities. The International Weight Pull Association promotes weight pulling and has three levels of "working dog" title certificates. The American Pulling Alliance sponsors events, as does the National Working Dog Association and the Global Pulling Alliance.

A similar sport is carting, in which the dog pulls a small cart, but weight is not a factor in carting. Carting shows off skill rather than strength. Many breeds who were originally bred as draft animals, such as Bernese Mountain Dogs and Rottweilers, participate and earn titles in carting today. Many dogs can enjoy learning how to pull a cart even if they are not traditional carting breeds.

Northern breeds may also enjoy carting, especially when there's no snow.

HARNESSES

If you decide to try your hand at carting, be aware that different harnesses are used for different kinds of carting. Dogs who pull sleds in the snow need a different type of harness than dogs pulling small carts. If you want your dog to pull you in addition to a small cart, you may need another type of harness. The common harness that you might use instead of a collar and lead is not appropriate for any kind of carting or pulling.

Safety
at Home
and Away

Your dog can (and will want to) share many of the foods you eat and, as long as you don't overdo it, that's fine. If you're cooking for your dog, you'll be using human-grade ingredients and that's good, too, but there are some foods that humans enjoy that are harmful to canines.

DID YOU KNOW? For the same reasons that you want to avoid giving your dog chocolate, also avoid coffee, tea, and soft drinks with caffeine.

At the top of the list is chocolate. It's hard to believe that something we enjoy so much can't be shared with our dogs, but chocolate contains theobromine and caffeine, both of which can be fatal to a dog. The darker the chocolate, the greater the danger. The American Animal Hospital Association says that just 2-3 ounces of baking chocolate can kill a medium-sized dog, but it would take 1-1½ pounds of milk chocolate to have that same affect. White chocolate has almost no theobromine.

While not a food, another product to be wary of is cocoa mulch. This mulch smells like chocolate and contains theobromine and caffeine. Puppies, and some adult dogs, will put almost anything in their mouths, and they may find it great fun to chew on a piece of this mulch. Keep an eye on your dog or, better still, don't use cocoa mulch.

Depending on the amount and type of chocolate ingested, symptoms can include increased heart rate, tremors, vomiting, diarrhea, increased thirst, and lethargy. Large enough amounts of chocolate can result in death. Don't panic if your dog gets the occasional dropped M & M, but if your dog devours a bag of chocolate chips or several squares of baking chocolate, get him to your veterinarian immediately.

Giving your dog cooked egg in any form is fine, but avoid raw egg white, which contains avidin, a protein that binds up the B vitamin biotin so that the dog can't use it. Cooking the white changes the avidin so that it can no longer bind to the biotin.

No one wants a dog with onion or garlic breath, but that's not the main reason to avoid these members of the allium family. Both raw and cooked onion and onion powder can damage red blood cells and cause hemolytic anemia. Symptoms include vomiting, weakness, and pale gums. Once again, garlic flavoring or a small piece of onion is nothing to worry about, but if your dog consumes an entire clove of garlic or an onion, it's time for the veterinarian.

It's okay to toss your dog the occasional tortilla chip, but skip the guacamole and don't let your dog eat an entire avocado. There's a real danger of the avocado pit causing intestinal blockage, and too much avocado can lead to pancreatitis.

Macadamia nuts are a tasty snack with cocktails, but resist sharing with your dog. Depending on how many nuts a dog eats, the dog may show weakness, tremors, or vomiting. If a dog eats a large portion, his back legs will become paralyzed within twelve to twenty-four hours. The dog will also have a mild fever and may have an upset stomach. His front legs may be mildly affected, but the back legs won't work at all.

The good news is that this paralysis goes away within seventy-two hours and there are no lingering effects. The bad news is that, because of the time lag between eating the nuts and the onset of the paralysis, some dogs may be misdiagnosed and euthanized. So, keep the macadamia nuts out of your dog's reach or, better yet, switch to cashews.

Both grapes and raisins can cause kidney failure in dogs. While one or two grapes or raisins probably won't cause a problem, the amount that can cause trouble really isn't known. Play it safe and never let your dog eat grapes or raisins.

You might think that it would be OK to give your dog some food with mold on it rather than throw it away, but you'd be wrong. Some molds contain mycotoxins that can cause muscle tremors, convulsions, and loss of muscle control, and these symptoms can last for several days. If you won't eat it, don't give it to your dog.

If you love to bake, especially breads, keep that dough out of your dog's reach. If ingested, the dough can continue to rise in the dog's stomach due to his body heat. In addition to pain and possibly bloat and vomiting, the dough produces ethanol as it rises, which can poison your dog. If your dog eats a pan of dough, don't wait. Get to your veterinarian immediately.

Xylitol is an artificial sweetener that, in dogs, can cause hypoglycemia, with symptoms of depression, loss of coordination, and seizures. Xylitol can also lead to liver failure. Xylitol is found in sugar-free gum and mints, but it can also be purchased in bulk for baking. If you use xylitol instead of sugar, keep it away from your dog.

You might think that once you've finished a piece of corn on the cob, the cob would make a great chew for your dog. Banish the thought. Corncobs are indigestible, and, if your dog swallows a large chunk, it can lead to intestinal blockage but won't show up on an x-ray. I speak from experience. Our first dog, who weighed in at 110 pounds, was occasionally given a nibble of a cob. She was dainty about it and seemed to chew it with no ill effects. Our first Corgi, at about 25 pounds, was nicknamed "Jaws." When offered a bite of corncob, he opened wide and bit off a large chunk, which, apparently, he swallowed whole. Two months (not a typo) later, he was definitely not well, so he ended up at the vet's for a few days, during which time he explosively passed the corn cob. So, play it safe. No corncobs, ever.

Nicotine is not technically a food, but it's deadly if ingested. Symptoms include vomiting, diarrhea, twitching, and shallow respiration leading to collapse and death. Keep all cigarettes, cigars, snuff, and chewing tobacco away from your dog. Empty ashtrays before your dog can get to the butts.

Cooked bones, even beef bones, can splinter and, when swallowed, puncture the intestines. Give only raw bones to your dog and, after two or three days, take them away. By then, they will have dried out and be just as likely to splinter as cooked bones.

There are hundreds of plants that are dangerous to your dog, but with just a little caution, you can keep your dog safe. Several plants commonly used around Christmastime, for instance, have poisonous parts that you need to be aware of. All parts of mistletoe are poisonous—leaves, stems, and berries—but it's the berries that are the worst. Mistletoe berries can be fatal if your dog ingests even a few. If you have mistletoe in your home and your dog is vomiting, has diarrhea, has seizures, or falls into a coma, get him to your veterinarian immediately. Play it safe and buy a nice artificial cluster. They look quite real and eliminate a potential source of trouble.

Holly berries can cause an upset stomach, seizures, and loss of balance, so again play it safe and invest in some artificial holly. It will last throughout the season, and you can use it again next year.

Poinsettias have always gotten a bad rap as being poisonous, but they're not nearly as bad as mistletoe and holly. The leaves, stems, and sap can cause irritation, and the sap can cause blindness if it gets into the eyes. If your dog chews on a poinsettia, he could suffer from vomiting and diarrhea. You don't have to eliminate poinsettias from your decorating scheme, but put them in the center of a table, on a mantel, or somewhere else out of the reach of curious pups. Again, lovely artificial ones are always an option.

Mistletoe

The Christmas rose can cause vomiting and diarrhea, as well as affecting the heart. Last, but not least, ivy can cause vomiting, diarrhea, muscular spasms, and paralysis.

Moving on from holiday plants, boxwood and yew are both very dangerous to dogs. Boxwood can cause heart failure, and yew has poisonous berries and foliage. Eating the berries can cause cramping and vomiting, and eating the foliage can cause sudden death, with no symptoms. If you have boxwood on your property, or a yew tree, get rid of both before you get a dog.

Another plant I would never have in my yard is oleander. Oleander is very toxic, and all parts of the plant are poisonous, particularly the leaves, which contain toxins known as glycosides. Symptoms are gastrointestinal problems, cardiac problems, and hypothermia; in some cases, it can cause sudden death.

Iris, tulip, and daffodil bulbs are poisonous, but unless you have a puppy who is in the digging phase, you can enjoy the flowers without much danger. If you have a terrier who may enjoy digging throughout his entire life and may dig up a bulb or two chasing a rodent, use a little more caution.

Several years ago, we had two apple trees in our yard. The apples were on the small side but were edible. All of our Corgis loved lying in the yard and munching apple after apple. Apple seeds contain cyanide, as do cherry and peach pits. I have no idea how many apple seeds a pet has to eat to be poisoned, but it must be quite a few because none of my dogs ever had an adverse reaction. Peach pits, being larger, would be more of a threat and could also cause an intestinal blockage.

Rhododendron, philodendron, marigolds, hydrangea, hemlock, and rhubarb can all be harmful. Most of my dogs have ignored plantings in the yard, and puppies are most likely to get into danger by chewing on a plant. One of our Corgis enjoyed chewing lilac branches when she was young; fortunately, lilacs are nontoxic.

Another growth that may be harmful to pets is one you might overlook because it's not always visible and not something you'd plant yourself. It's mushrooms. Many are totally harmless, but many are harmful, and, unless you're a student of mushrooms, you won't know the difference until it's too late. The ASPCA reports that, depending on the mushroom, these fungi can cause kidney or liver damage or serious neurological consequences; some types of mushroom can be fatal. Don't let your pets snack on mushrooms and remove any mushrooms you see sprouting up in your yard.

If you're planning to add a new plant to your yard, ask the folks at the nursery about any parts of the plant that may be poisonous. There are too many hazardous plants to list them all here, but you can find a comprehensive list of toxic plants by searching "poisonous plants" on the ASPCA's website (www.aspca.org).

Flowering hemlock

There are many common household products that can be harmful to your dog. Generally speaking, keep all cleaning products as well as all medicines and drugs, insecticides, rodenticides, and fertilizers away from your pet.

Antifreeze is particularly deadly for your dog. It contains ethylene glycol, which has a sweet taste, so dogs think it's a treat. It's not. It can be fatal if your dog gets even a tablespoon of it. If your dog has access to your garage, be alert to any drips or spills of antifreeze. Symptoms of antifreeze poisoning include vomiting, depression, seizures, and coma. If you suspect your dog has swallowed some antifreeze, get him to the veterinarian immediately.

While kerosene use is not as common now as it once was, many people enjoy the

DID YOU KNOW?

If your dog ingests a toxin, check with your veterinarian first before inducing vomiting. Vomiting is generally encouraged with a toxic food or plant, and vomiting may also be suggested with certain drugs and insecticides, but many household products will just cause more damage to the esophagus if regurgitated. Always check with your veterinarian before trying any treatment.

BEWARE BATTERIES

Batteries are not good chew toys. Keep batteries out of reach, especially if you have a puppy.

decorative properties of kerosene lamps, especially during winter holidays. You can enjoy your kerosene lamps, but keep the kerosene supply locked away from curious canines. If your dog does get into the kerosene, get him to the vet immediately. Don't encourage vomiting because the kerosene will just do more damage to the esophagus and may also get into the lungs. If your dog gets the fuel on his skin, wash him thoroughly.

Laundry detergent is another product to keep away from your dog. Pods can be especially dangerous because their compact size makes it easy for a dog to grab one. Spurting liquid can harm the eyes as well as being toxic if swallowed. Bleach is another hazard. If bleach splashes on your dog, wash the dog thoroughly. If bleach gets into his eyes, rinse his eyes immediately and go to the veterinarian.

THE MEDICINE CABINET

Acetaminophen, the drug in Tylenol and other pain relievers, can cause serious liver damage in dogs. Never give acetaminophen to your dog. It is generally OK to give your dog aspirin for pain; ask your vet for the correct dosage based on your dog's weight. If your dog eats an entire bottle of aspirin, however, call your vet immediately.

Don't give human antihistamines and decongestants to your dog unless under your vet's direction. Your veterinarian may prescribe one of these medicines, such as Benadryl, for your dog, but she'll prescribe it in the correct dosage for your dog. Generally, keep all human medicines away from your dog and do not attempt to treat your dog on your own.

If you suspect that your dog has ingested a drug in your home, get him to your veterinarian and take the medicine container with you; this will give the vet a head start on knowing how to treat your dog.

Citrus oils are found in many products, including shampoos, and large concentrations of them can be toxic to your dog. Yes, you can use a dog shampoo that contains citrus oils, but don't let your dog lick or swallow it. If you use citrus oils for aromatherapy, keep those oils away from your dog.

Both naphthalene and paradichlorobenzene are toxic. Naphthalene is found in toilet-bowl deodorizers, mothballs, moth crystals, and moth cakes. Paradichlorobenzene is found in diaper-pail, toilet-bowl, and restroom deodorizers as well as in mothballs, moth crystals, and moth cakes.

Keep your dog away from these products or anything containing one of these ingredients: amitraz, anticoagulants, borate (found in boric acid and borax), bromethalin, DEET, ivermectin, metaldehyde (a slug and snail bait), pyrethrin, rotenone, and strychnine. You may find some of these ingredients in products that you use for your dog, but they are in doses appropriate to your pet. Ivermectin, for instance, is in many heartworm products. Amitraz may be in a flea or tick medicine. Never let your dog chew on a flea or tick collar, and always follow directions for all medicines.

If you suspect your dog has ingested anything poisonous, whether a food, plant, drug, or cleaning product, and you can't reach your veterinarian and don't have an emergency veterinary clinic in your area, there are two twenty-four-hour hotlines that you can call for help. Pet Poison Helpline charges a per-incident fee and can be reached at 855-764-7661. The ASPCA Animal Poison Control Center (APCC) also charges a consultation fee and can be reached at 888-426-4435.

BACKYARD CAUTION

Many lawn and garden products can be harmful to dogs, so read labels carefully. If your goal is a picture-perfect lawn, carefully consider your decision to get a dog in the first place.

No matter what kind of identification you use for your dog, don't rely solely on those methods to get your dog back should he become lost. While you hope that this will never happen, you can't waste any time if it does.

Make fliers. Include a clear photo of your dog on a contrasting background. Your dog may look adorable on a pile of pillows, but could a stranger tell what your dog really looks like from that picture? Try to have a good full-body photo of your dog. In addition to the photo, include your phone number, the general area where your dog was lost, and your dog's sex and age. It may be more helpful to say "puppy" or "older dog with gray muzzle" than to give the exact age in years. Even if you are including a color photo, describe your dog's coloration. If the only photo you have is in black and white, describe your dog's color in terms everyone will understand. Instead of saying "tri-color," say "black, brown, and white." Offer a reward, but don't specify the amount on the poster.

Post your fliers on community bulletin boards and at local veterinarians' offices. Hand them out door to door. Notify your police department and animal control, and ask your neighbors to keep an eye out for your dog.

Call area veterinarians. Maybe your dog was hit by a car and taken to an animal hospital. Call again. Check the local shelter. Don't

rely on phone calls, and don't rely on having someone at a shelter call you. Go in person. As clearly as you may describe your dog, the person listening may be picturing a different dog entirely. A fluffy white dog can mean many things to different people, as can words like "small," "medium," and "large." Even if you mention a specific breed, a person may think that your Bichon Frise is a Poodle. Or you may have a mixed breed that doesn't really look like either parent. A friend of mine has a Doberman–Malamute cross that looks quite a bit like a German Shepherd Dog.

Look at the dogs who have been picked up as strays, and check every day. Show the shelter staff pictures of your dog and leave a photo for the next shift.

Visit all the shelters in your area. Dogs can travel amazing distances. It's also possible that someone could pick up your dog and then either release him further away or lose him again. Years ago, a neighbor's German Shepherd Dog got loose from the yard and was found an hour and a half later—more than 10 miles away. This isn't always the case, but it can happen.

Use social media. Many rescue organizations post dogs they've found on Facebook, and often people who've found a dog will post. Post your flier on your own page and ask people to share it. Post on community forums and keep checking to see if anyone reports seeing your dog. A friend of mine had a dog who was missing for more than two weeks before she saw her dog's picture on Facebook, posted as a dog at the local shelter, after which he was quickly reunited with his owner.

If you have a local newspaper, run an ad in the lost and found column and ask local radio stations to announce your lost dog. Many times, these announcements are free both in newspapers and on the radio. Make sure you also read the ads placed in the "found" column.

I hope you never need this information, but if you do, it may help you get your dog home safe and sound. Don't give up too soon. Someone may be feeding a "stray" or have actually taken your dog in and not yet seen an ad or a poster, especially if your dog has traveled a distance.

98 Travel Tips

While you may never travel across the country with your dog, you will need to make at least some trips by car, even if it's just to the vet's office or grooming salon. Most dogs have no problem with riding in a car, and many enjoy it, happy to jump in for a ride anytime. Some dogs are afraid of cars, though, and some may get carsick the first few times they are taken for a ride.

Most dogs will get into a car with no hesitation, but if your dog doesn't like cars, you'll need to work slowly to get him used to the idea. First, open the doors on both sides of the car so that your dog sees that it's not an enclosed space. Encourage him with treats to get in the car and then lead him out again. Don't try to keep him in the car, and don't shut the doors. Gradually increase the time that the dog is in the car and then shut one door while leaving the other open.

When your dog seems calm and accepting of the car, shut both doors and just sit for a few minutes without starting the car. This conditioning can take up to two weeks or even more, but be patient. Don't rush the process or force your dog; it will just end up taking longer. Keep sessions short and happy.

When you can finally start the engine, keep that first trip very short, maybe just the length of your driveway. If you have a helper, he or she can give the dog treats and help to take his mind off the road.

Even if your dog loves car rides, never travel with your dog loose in the car. A loose dog in a car can be a real danger if there's an accident, and he's likely to end up going through the windshield. If a dog manages to be unhurt in an accident, he may escape the car and become lost or injured. The best way for your dog to travel is in a crate in the back

of the car, with the crate on the floor against the front seats or securely fastened to the seat. A good choice, but not the best, is a harness that attaches to the car's seat-belt system.

It's hard to leave your dog behind when you're on vacation, and many people travel with their dogs all the time. It's a little extra work, but it's nice to have your dog with you. Here are some things to think about:

Whether you're traveling to a dog event or are on vacation, carry water from home for your dog. If you're going to be gone for an extended period, gradually add water from your destination to the water you've brought with you so there's not a sudden change. Travel with enough of your dog's usual food, too. A food that's common in your local pet-supply store may not be common at your destination. Travel can be stressful for your dog, so try to keep things like food a constant. If you cook for your dog or feed raw, you'll need a good cooler so that the food doesn't spoil.

Carry food and water dishes for your dog or at least his water bowl and some paper plates that you can serve his food on and then

throw away. This can be convenient if you're feeding a meal on the road or are camping.

If your dog is on any medication, make sure you have enough with you for the entire trip. Carry your dog's vaccination record with you as well, especially if you are traveling across state lines or into another country. It's a good idea to have a small first-aid kit with you, too. Carry paper towels as well as regular towels in case your dog gets wet or muddy.

As you travel, you may be planning to stop at tourist attractions along the way. Consider your dog before you make those stops. Some attractions have kennel facilities, but many do not. Do not plan to leave your dog in the car. A dog in a car is never a good idea, especially in the summer. Even with the windows down, the interior temperature of a car can reach deadly levels, and keeping the windows down could mean he will escape or be stolen. Parking in the shade is no guarantee that your dog will be safe, either. As the sun moves, so does the shade, and your car could end up with no shade at all. A dog's cooling system is not very efficient, and stress decreases that efficiency. It doesn't take long for a dog to overheat and die. If you can't leave your dog in your hotel room or at a kennel, skip the attraction.

Another thing to think about if you're taking your dog with you on vacation is where you'll be staying. If you're staying with friends or relatives, make sure they know ahead of time that you'll be bringing your dog. Even if they know and like your dog, they may not be prepared to have the dog in their home. Think about what your destination is like. Will there be room to exercise your dog? Are there other dogs? Are there children? If your dog has grown up with children, he'll likely be fine, but if a dog isn't used to children, they can make him nervous and uncomfortable.

If you're staying at a hotel, or if you'll be staying at various hotels as you travel, make sure your dog is welcome before you check in. AAA offers members a book of pet-friendly hotels, motels, and campgrounds, *Traveling with Your Pet*, which is a great starting place. Just remember to always call and confirm that

> **HOTEL HINT**
> If possible, try to stay in rooms that open onto an inside corridor, rather than to the outdoors. Then, if your dog manages to get out the door, he's still in a contained area, not in a parking lot or on a busy road.

dogs are welcome because places change ownership and rules can change. Also, find out ahead of time if the hotel or inn charges extra for dogs. Some places have a one-time pet fee; some charge extra for each night. These fees may be very reasonable, or it may be cheaper to leave your dog at home in a boarding kennel or with a pet sitter.

The same rules apply for camping. Make sure that campgrounds allow dogs and, if so, what they require. State and federal camping areas will require proof that your dog has been vaccinated against rabies, so don't forget that paperwork.

Wherever you stay, make sure you are a responsible owner. Keep your dog under control at all times and pick up after your dog no matter where you are. If you're staying in a hotel or motel room, crate your dog when you're not in the room with him. When you leave, turn on a radio or television so that the noise masks outside noises that might cause your dog to bark.

When I travel, my dogs love to join me on the bed, but housekeeping won't appreciate dog hair all over the bedspread. Travel with a couple of sheets so that you can cover the bed with them. This also keeps the spread clean if your dog has muddy paws. Don't bathe your dog in a hotel bathroom and, if your dog has dirty feet, wipe them off with your own towels rather than using those supplied by the hotel. Carry a piece of plastic to put under food and water dishes to catch any spills.

If you think your dog will bark at or be stressed by the housekeeping staff, hang out the "do not disturb" sign. You can make your own bed, and, if you want clean towels, you can ask at the front desk or make arrangements to leave the dirty ones outside the door, and housekeeping will leave you clean ones.

Flying may be another mode of transportation to consider. If you have a small dog, you may be able to put him in an under-the-seat carrier, but many airlines limit the number of pets allowed on a flight, so don't assume you can bring your dog on board. For larger dogs, the only option is the baggage compartment. Many people fly with their dogs with no problems, but you do need to be aware of all the regulations, which vary from carrier to carrier, and you need to plan ahead. You can't just show up at the airport with your dog and a crate.

Another consideration when flying is whether or not there is quarantine at your

destination. Britain used to have a six-month quarantine period, which they no longer have if your dog meets certain vaccination requirements. Hawaii's quarantine time has recently been shortened. Know the regulations and be prepared to follow them before you book your tickets.

A company that handles shipping animals is Animal Land Pet Movers (www.petmovers.com). They've been in business since 1998 and are licensed by the United States Department of Agriculture as intermediate animal handlers. While this might not be useful for a vacation, this service would be especially helpful if you were moving across country or overseas. Travel restrictions have eased for many countries, but there is still a lot of paperwork and many requirements that must be met. According to their website, Animal Land will not only arrange all flights, but will make sure all international requirements are met, including import permits and shot records.

TRANSPORTATION TIP

If you enjoy traveling by either rail or bus, you're out of luck if you want to bring your dog with you. Amtrak doesn't allow dogs, nor does Greyhound, in spite of their name. Local trains and buses may allow dogs, but check first so that you don't risk being turned away.

99 Boarding Your Dog

Dogs become so much a part of the family that it seems only natural to take them with us when we go on vacation. Sometimes that just isn't practical. I can't easily take my dogs on a visit overseas to London or across the country to visit my in-laws. And, once in a while, it's nice to go somewhere and not build my schedule around my dogs.

When our dogs are left behind, they're at a reputable boarding kennel. I like kennels because the dogs are kept in an enclosed area. When I go away, I don't want to worry that a house sitter or pet sitter has left a gate open or that a Corgi will scoot out the front door as a caretaker comes in. Plus, most kennel operators know enough about animals to be able to tell if a dog is sick or hurt. They see their charges more times throughout the day and can pick up on odd behavior that may indicate a problem. A pet sitter who only comes in twice a day may miss that.

As someone who used to own a boarding kennel, I can say that more than 99 percent of the animals settled in and were content to be there. Your dog may look pathetic when you drop him off, but, five minutes later, he'll be wagging his tail and happily accepting a treat. Still, a successful boarding experience depends on communication between you and the kennel operator.

First, have a copy of your dog's shot record. Kennel operators want to make sure that all dogs in their care have the necessary vaccinations and that there's no danger they'll either catch or spread a disease. In addition to proof of rabies and distemper shots, many kennels also ask for a bordetella, or "kennel cough," shot.

If your dog has any problems or is on any medication, let the kennel staff know and make sure you supply whatever medicine is needed. If your dog eats a special food, supply it—and don't ask for a discount on your boarding bill because you are supplying your own food. You are paying for safe care.

Put all medication and feeding instructions in writing for the kennel staff. This will save you from trying to remember everything in the flurry of dropping off your dog, and the kennel staff will have your instructions on hand even if the same person is not always taking care of your dog. Most kennels will ask for your veterinarian's name and number and for an emergency contact; if they don't ask, offer it.

When I leave my dogs, I request that anything out of the ordinary be treated aggressively. I'd rather pay a veterinary bill for something minor than let a small problem go untreated and turn into something serious. If I'm going to be away for an extended amount of time, I let my veterinarian know that I authorize him to do whatever is necessary to treat my dog in my absence. I don't want the veterinarian to hesitate because he can't reach me.

Visit the kennel before you make a reservation for your dog. The dog runs should be in good shape—clean, with no protruding wires or slivers of wood. The kennel should not smell dirty. Kennels may smell like animals, but they should not smell of urine or feces. If there's a separate exercise area, it also should be clean. Look around the indoor and outdoor areas. How are the gates locked? Is there a security fence around the runs? Do the animals have access to fresh water? How often are the dogs let out?

Ask if the kennel offers any grooming services. I like to arrange for my dogs to be bathed before I pick them up if I'm gone for an extended amount of time. I don't care how clean a kennel is, there's still a kennel smell that dogs pick up. Also, a bath will catch any fleas that might have found your dog. Good kennels fight fleas and work to keep the dogs' areas clean, but there's no guarantee that someone else's dog won't bring in some fleas.

Most kennels will let you leave your dog's bed, but be warned that if the dog gets bored or anxious and decides to chew, he may destroy his bed. A Dachshund I boarded once totally destroyed a beautiful—and expensive—wicker bed. Another dog, a Doberman, ripped open his beanbag bed, filling his run with Styrofoam "beans." Towels are a safer, cheaper alternative. Depending on the size of your dog and the size of the area

in which he will be kept, you might consider leaving his crate at the kennel to give your dog a bit more of a sense of security.

Some animal hospitals offer boarding, and some owners are very comfortable with that because there's a veterinarian right there if your dog should become ill. Most hospitals, though, are not specifically set up to care for boarding animals. Sick animals are the priority, and your dog may not get as much attention as you'd like. There may not even be outdoor runs, or your dog may only get a short walk twice a day. Boarding at a veterinarian's office makes sense if you have a dog who needs certain treatments each day; for instance, insulin for a diabetic dog. If your veterinarian does offer boarding, get the details on how and where your dog will be kept before you make your decision.

Once you've chosen a place to board your dog, harden your heart to your pet's pathetic looks as you leave him behind. Enjoy your vacation, knowing that your pet will be well cared for.

Will your dog be walked with other dogs?

A pet sitter can be a good alternative to a kennel, especially if your dog becomes anxious in strange places or if your dog is older and needs more attention than a kennel can give. An older dog may also get disoriented in a strange place and not adjust well to a kennel, or that older pet may have a bit of arthritis and be uncomfortable in a kennel.

Another benefit to a pet sitter is that it will make your house look like someone is home while you are away. There will be lights on and maybe a car in the driveway at different times. A pet sitter may also be willing to take in the mail, collect newspapers, and water houseplants.

If you live in a larger metropolitan area, you may be able to find a pet sitter through a professional pet-sitting organization, such as Pet Sitters International (www.petsit.com) or the National Association of Professional Pet Sitters (www.petsitters.org). There may also be a local company in your area. Make sure that any professional sitter is bonded and has insurance.

Ask about pet sitting at your veterinarian's office. Sometimes vet techs also pet sit, which gives you the added bonus of having someone with medical training taking care of your dog. Ask dog-owning friends, who may be able to refer you to their pet sitters. Don't be afraid to ask for references. You might have a friend or neighbor who's willing to help out as well, but don't choose him or her just out of convenience. The teen next door may love animals, but is she responsible? Can you trust her to remember your dog's medicine? Will she always remember to latch the gate to the yard?

What do you want the sitter to do? A sitter who stays at your house will likely charge more than one who just drops by a few times a day. If you want your sitter to schedule playtimes with your dog or take him for long walks, this may also cost more.

No matter who you hire, be specific in what you expect and put everything in writing. A professional sitter may have a contract, but there may be things you need to modify on a basic contract. Don't assume anything. Write out when your dog is to be fed and how much. Are there supplements? Medicines? If you have multiple dogs, can they be fed together? If not, tell your sitter how you manage feeding times. If your sitter is living in, how do you feel about your dog getting human food? A sitter may routinely give her own dog pizza crusts, but you may be horrified at the idea. Make your rules clear. Is your dog allowed on all furniture or only on the old chair in the corner? Tell your sitter.

Post emergency numbers, a number where you can be reached, and your veterinarian's number. Tell your veterinarian before you go that the pet sitter has the authority to seek treatment for your dog and that you will pay all bills.

Last, your sitter needs to come to your home and meet your dog before you go away. Depending on your dog, you may want to have the sitter come more than once, and it might also be a good idea for the sitter to visit once when you're not home to see how your dog reacts when you're not there. Make sure that the sitter and your dog are comfortable with each other. You are depending on that person to take care of your dog in your absence. If the sitter seems at all uncertain or nervous around your dog, find another sitter or choose a kennel.

Registries
American Kennel Club
www.akc.org

United Kennel Club
www.ukcdogs.com

Canadian Kennel Club
www.ckc.ca

Adoption Sites
Petfinder
www.petfinder.com

Petcha
www.petcha.com

Medical Sites
Note: These sites are for reference only, to help you understand a particular disease or to find a particular practitioner, such as an acupuncturist. Do not rely on the Internet to diagnose and treat ailments in your dog. Your veterinarian is your safest bet for keeping your dog healthy.

Purdue University College of Veterinary Medicine
www.vet.purdue.edu

PetMD
www.petmd.com

WebMD Pets
pets.webmd.com

VetStreet
www.vetstreet.com

American Veterinary Medical Association: www.avma.org

American Veterinary Chiropractic Association
www.animalchiropractic.org

International Veterinary Acupuncture Society www.ivas.org

OptiGen
www.optigen.com

Poison Control Hotlines
ASPCA
Animal Poison Control Center
888-426-4435

Pet Poison Helpline
855-764-7661

Pet Sitters
National Association of Professional Pet Sitters
www.petsitters.org

Pet Sitters International
www.petsit.com

Conformation Shows
InfoDog
www.infodog.com

Performance Events
American Treibball Association
www.americantreibballassociation.org

United States Dog Agility Association
www.usdaa.com

North American Dog Agility Council
www.nadac.com

Dog on Course in North America
www.docna.com

UK Agility International
www.ukagilityinternational.com

North American Diving Dogs
www.northamericadivingdogs.com

DockDogs
www.dockdogs.com

Ultimate Air Dogs
www.ultimateairdogs.net

Canine Freestyle Federation
www.canine-freestyle.org

World Canine Freestyle Organization
www.worldcaninefreestyle.org

Dog Scouts of America
www.dogscouts.org.

International Weight Pull Association
www.iwpa.net

American Pulling Alliance
www.weightpull.com

National Working Dog Association
www.nwdak9.com

North American Hunting Dog Association www.navhda.org

Hunting Retriever Club
www.huntingretrieverclub.org

American Herding Breeds Association
www.ahba-herding.org

Australian Shepherd Trial Association
www.a-s-t-a.org

United States Border Collie Handlers' Association, Inc.
www.usbcha.com

American Border Collie Association
www.americanbordercollie.org

American Sighthound Field Organization
www.asfa.org

The National Greyhound Association
www.ngagreyhounds.com

The Midwest Skijorers Club
www.skijor.org

Barn Hunt Association
www.barnhunt.com

The American Working Terrier Association
www.awta.org

North American Flyball Association
www.flyball.org

National Association of Canine Scent Work
www.nacsw.net

Sport Detection Dog Association
www.sportingdetectiondogs.ca

Jack Russell Terrier Club of America
www.therealljackrussell.com

Therapy Work
Pet Partners
www.petpartners.org

Therapy Dogs International
www.tdi-dog.org

Index

All photos courtesy of Shutterstock except page 224 by Cathy Panebianco.

Front cover: Tomsickova Tatyana

Back cover: Eric Isselee

Backgrounds: james weston, zphoto

absolutimages, 89;; Adya, 47, 51; Africa Studio, 127, 152; alens, 180; Ermolaev Alexander, 25 (bottom), 113, 128; Kuznetsov Alexey, 179; Andresr, 7, 26; Medvedev Andrey, 66; anetapics, 17; Nina Anna, 96; apiguide, 132 (left); Aseph, 12; Inna Astakhova, 62, 118; baibaz, 132 (right); Javier Brosch, 88, 103; Joy Brown, 142; Ekaterina Brusnika: 215; Jayme Burrows, 213; Cat Act Art, 146; Diego Cervo, 86; Lars Christensen, 25 (top), 156; Nathan clifford, 59; WilleeCole Photography, 35, 41, 48, 108, 110, 147, 158, 176, 186; James Coleman, 106; Paul Cotney, 19; CREATISTA, 13; Linn Currie, 182; cynoclub, 18, 45, 52, 66, 123, 153, 168; DanyL, 71; Andy Dean Photography, 8; Ganna Demchenko, 136; elbud, 151; Sergey Fatin, 164; Tom Feist, 169, 170; Fly_dragonfly, 102, 119; Foto2rich, 134; GLYPHstock, 171; gori910, 87; gorillaimages, 14; Halfpoint, 160; Hannahmariah, 144; Nopphadol Hongsriphan, 30; Nicole Hrustyk, 189; Joerg Huettenhoelscher, 93; Hysteria, 197; ifong, 199; Imageman, 200 (right); IrinaK, 114 ; Eric Isselee, 6, 19, 21, 29, 40, 53, 54, 75, 92, 98, 126, 131, 140 (left), 149, 150, 152, 156, 161, 172, 173, 190; Jagodka, 18, 48, 49, 100, ; Rosa Jay, 10; JStaley401, 15, 105, 112; Aneta Jungerova, 57; Dmitry Kalinovsky, 181; Laila Kazakevica, 135; KITSANANAN, 200 (left); Rita Kochmarjova, 184, 185; Igor Kovalchuk, 201; Oksana Kuzmina, 97; lbomber, 32; Lenkadan, 196; llike, 70; Daleen Loest, 80; Blazej Lyjak, 36; Erik Lam, 4, 11, 56, 58 (left), 74, 82, 172, 178; Mackland, 177; Dorottya Mathe, 61, 122, 143; Sue McDonald, 88; michaeljung, 33; Mikadun, 206   ; miker, 195; MirasWonderland, 9; Monkey Business Images, 191; Nejron Photo, 22; Neonci, 77; N K, 20; NSC Photography, 192; Juan Carlos Nunez, 207; Okeanas, 19; Gridyakina Oleksandra, 203; osArt, 209; outc, 188; Zoltan Pataki, 145; Phase4Studios, 34; photka, 125; Photology1971, 74; picturepartners, 111; Picture-Pets, 175; Pixel Memoirs, 101; ANURAK PONGPATIMET, 27, 69, 99; pryzmat, 157; Victoria Rak, 171; Ratikova, 107; Chuck Rausin, 94; Raywoo, 194; rebeccaashworth, 24 (top); Reddogs, 165; karen roach, 138; Fesus Robert, 24 (bottom); Robynrg, 29; Rohappy, 139; Sarah2, 84; Carlos E. Santa Maria, 167; Susan Schmitz, 38, 43, 58 (right), 60, 72, 91, 121, 130, 134, 140 (right), 174; Seregraff, 13; Annette Shaff, 102, 104; sisqopote, 16; Ska_Zka, 137; Smart-foto, 133; Ljupco Smokovski, 63; SpeedKingz, 214; SSokolov, 117; Spasta, 138; steffiheufelder, 67; Straight 8 Photography, 37; Kuttelvaserova Stuchelova, 202; Sukpaiboonwat, 65; svry, 50; takayuki, 155; Barna Tanko, 163; ThamKC, 125; thka, 187; Jeff Thrower, 148; James_thungtong, 90; Anatoly Tiplyashin, 159; Vitaly Titov, 16, 95, 122; urbanbuzz, 204; Jne Valokuvaus, 68; violetblue, 115, 172; Vivenstock, 73; Sann von Mai, 76; Monika Vosahlova, 154; Vydrin, 129; Sally Wallis, 149; Filip Warulik, 166; Ivonne Wierink, 81; Monika Wisniewska, 208; Dora Zett, 78, 116, 158, 198

Susan M. Ewing has been "in dogs" for more than thirty-five years and has written close to a dozen dog books. She writes a bi-weekly pet column for the *Post-Journal* of Jamestown, New York, and has written for many national cat and dog publications. Her latest book, *American Pit Bull Terrier*, won a Maxwell Award from the Dog Writers' Association of America (DWAA). She is a member of DWAA and the Cat Writers' Association. She lives in Jamestown, New York, with her husband, Jim, and two Corgis, Rhiannon and Gael.